NAMIB

A SPECTACULAR JOURNEY

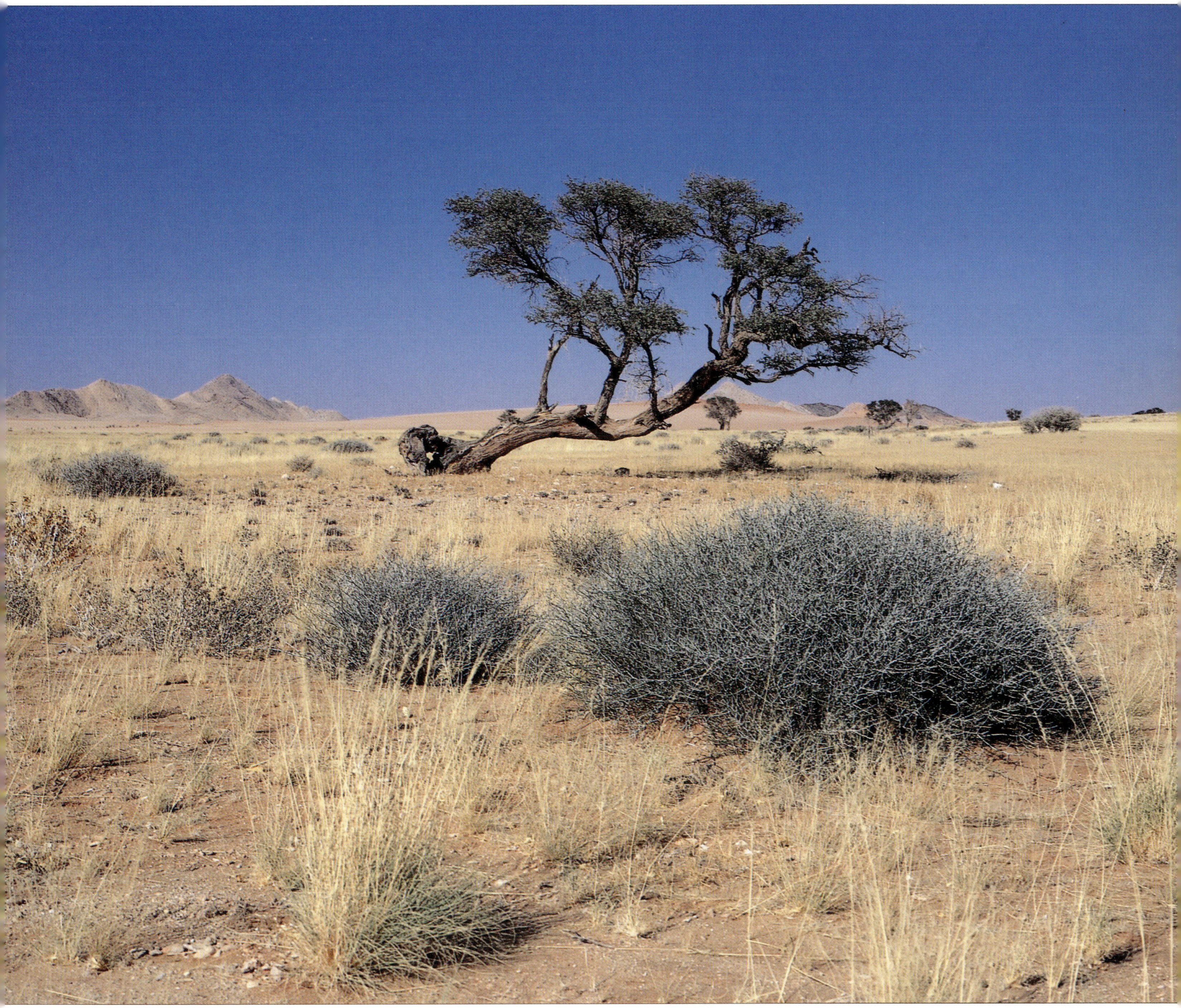

Rob Bickford
PUBLISHING

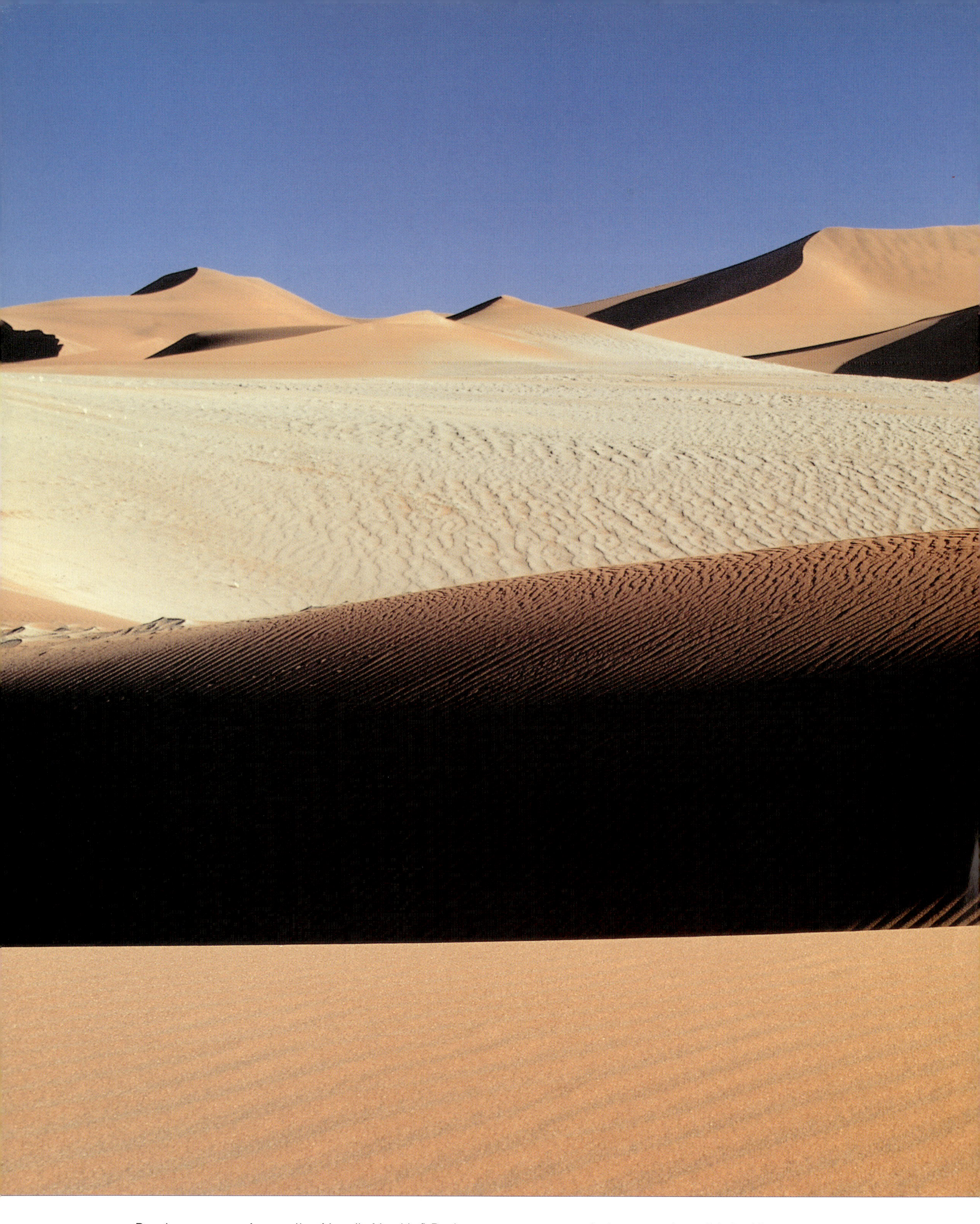

Previous page: Across the Namib Naukluft Park courageous acacia trees, such as this battler near Solitaire, defy the odds in surviving the Namib Desert's remorseless climatic conditions.

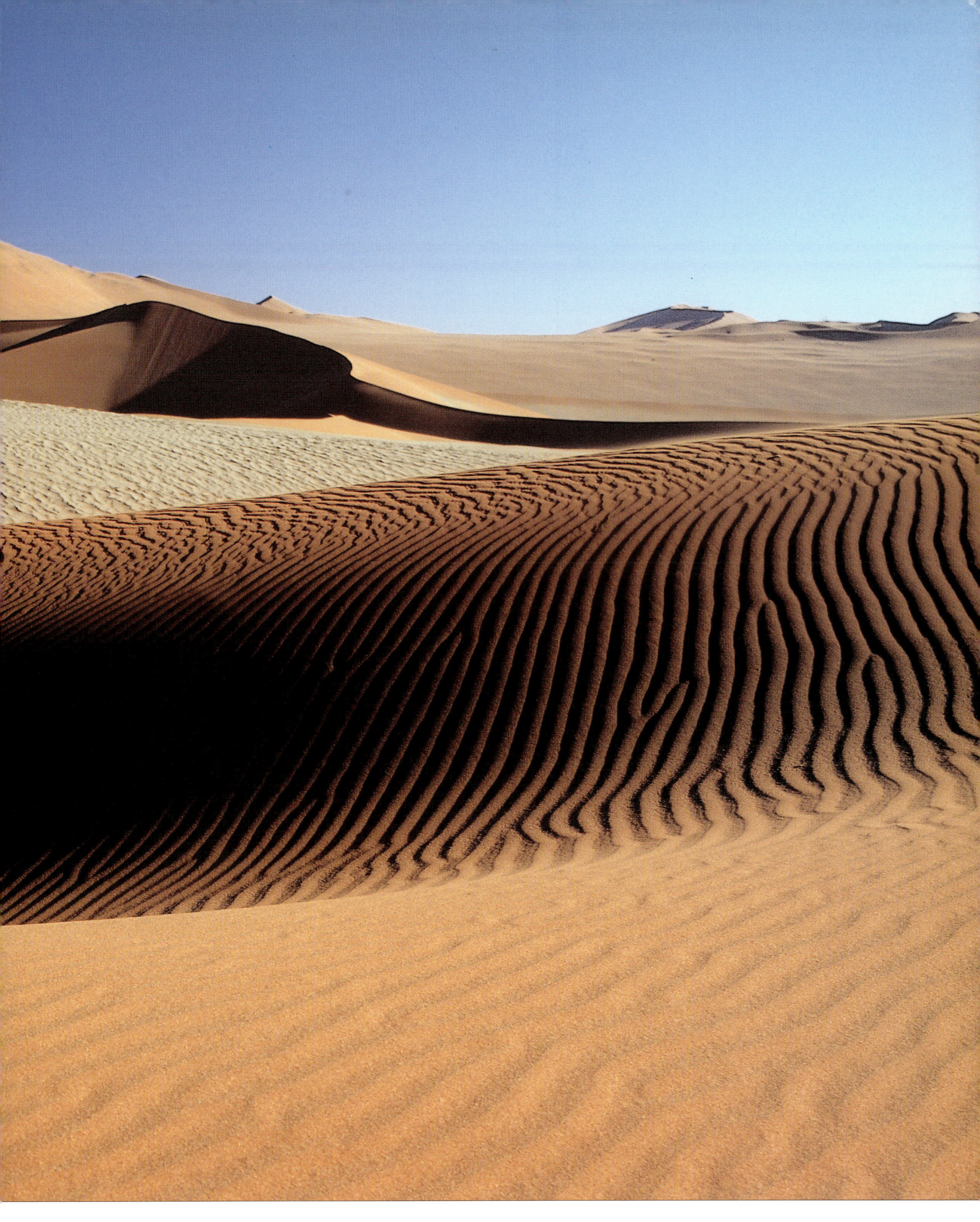

Light and shadow, sun and wind colour and craft the shapes and patterns of the mighty sand dunes at Sossusvlei to create an ever-changing, visual masterpiece.

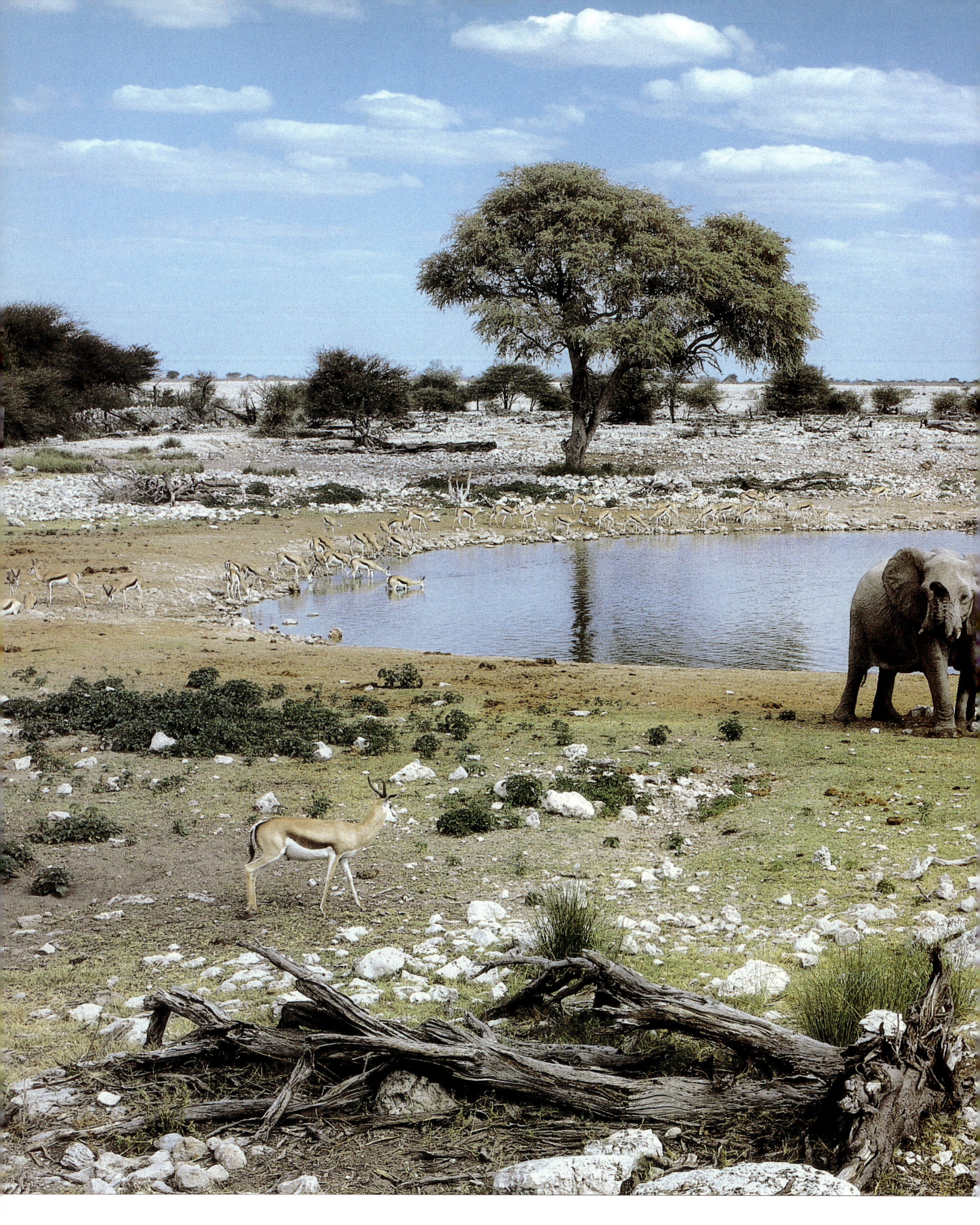

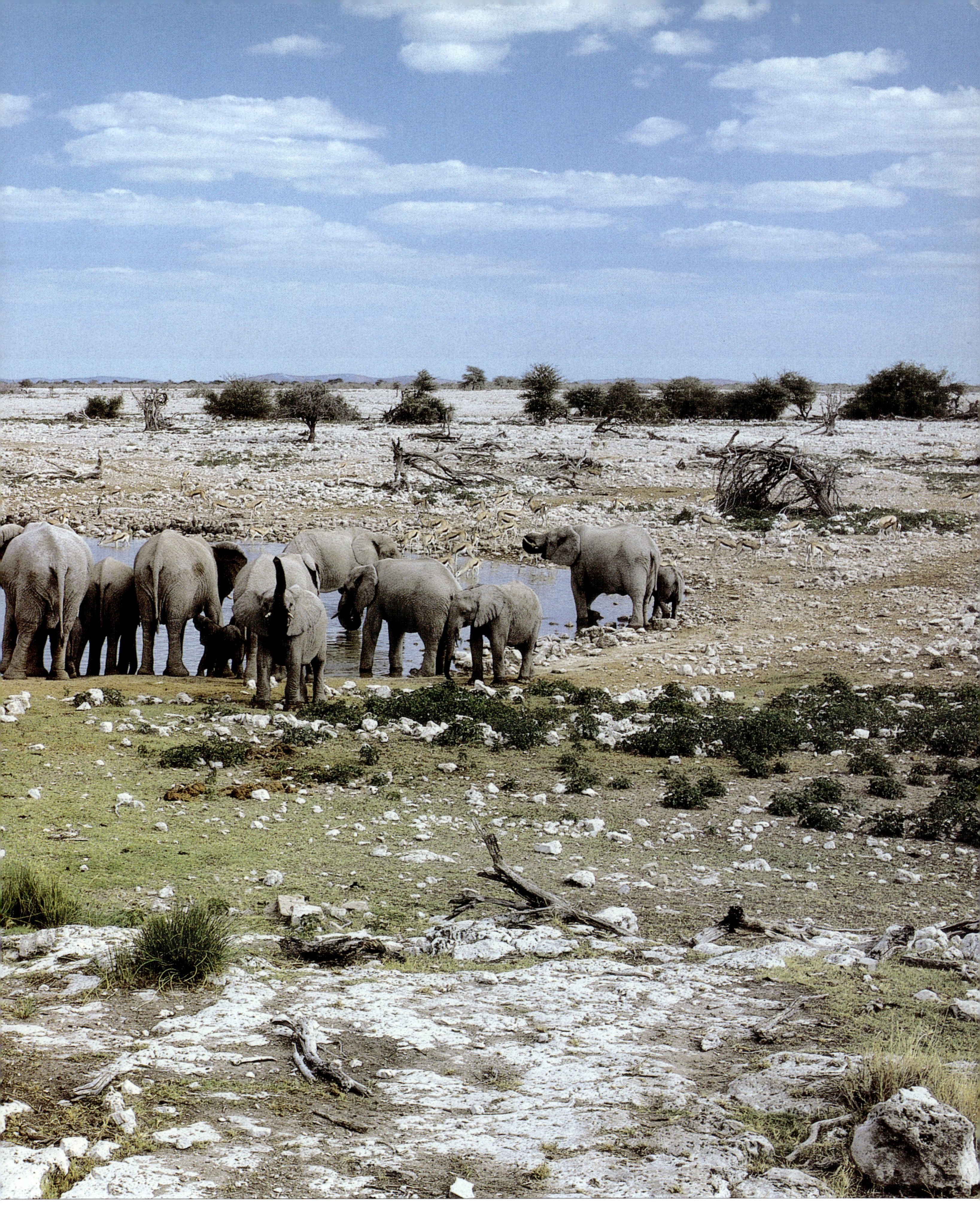

The waterhole at Etosha's Okaukuejo restcamp is a great place to view wildlife en masse. Thirsty patrons come and go 24 hours a day.

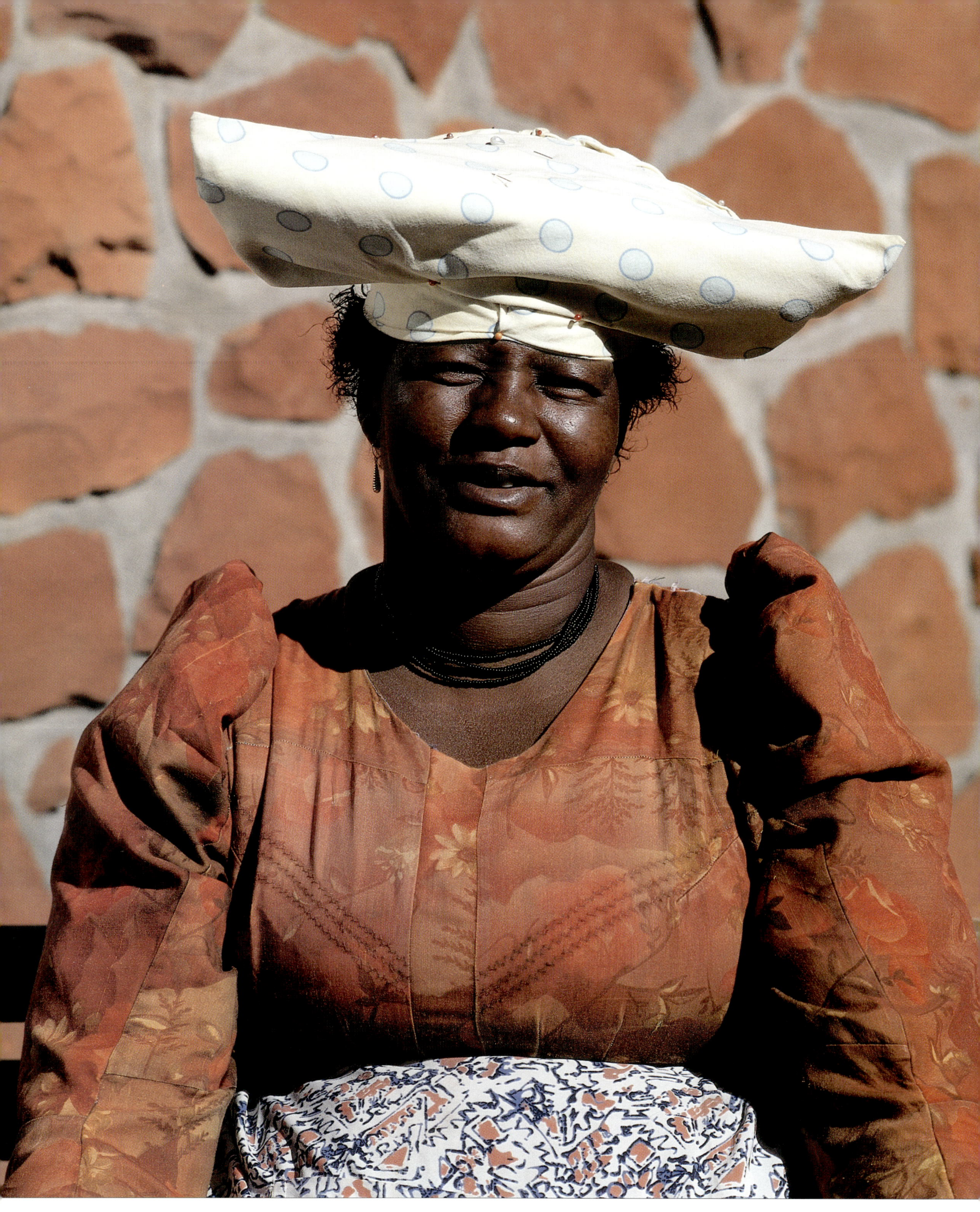

The everyday dress and headgear worn by Herero, Francesca, is derived from 19th century fashions. The Hereros' attire is every bit as grand as that of the Victorians they imitate.

CONTENTS

SOSSUSVLEI - VALLEY OF DUNES 13
SOSSUSVLEI - THE BIG RAINS 15
THE QUIVER TREE FOREST 19
THE DIAMOND GHOSTS OF KOLMANSKOP 21
KOLMANSKOP - THE ABANDONED TOWN 23
FISH RIVER CANYON 27
WILDLIFE ENCOUNTERS 31
ETOSHA NATIONAL PARK 45
WATERBERG PLATEAU 47
TWYFELFONTEIN – OUTDOOR MUSEUM 49
THE STONE AGE SAN MAN 50
NATURE'S HAND IN EARTH'S HISTORY 53
FEATHERED INHABITANTS 57
COLOUR AND CHARACTER 58
CAPE CROSS AND SEAL RESERVE 63
MOONSCAPE AND MIRABILIS 65
COLONIAL CHARM IN COASTAL TOWNS 67
OUT AND ABOUT 71
WINDHOEK - CAPITAL CITY 72
A MODERN COUNTRY 75
NAMIBIA - A SPECTACULAR JOURNEY 76
MAP OF NAMIBIA 77

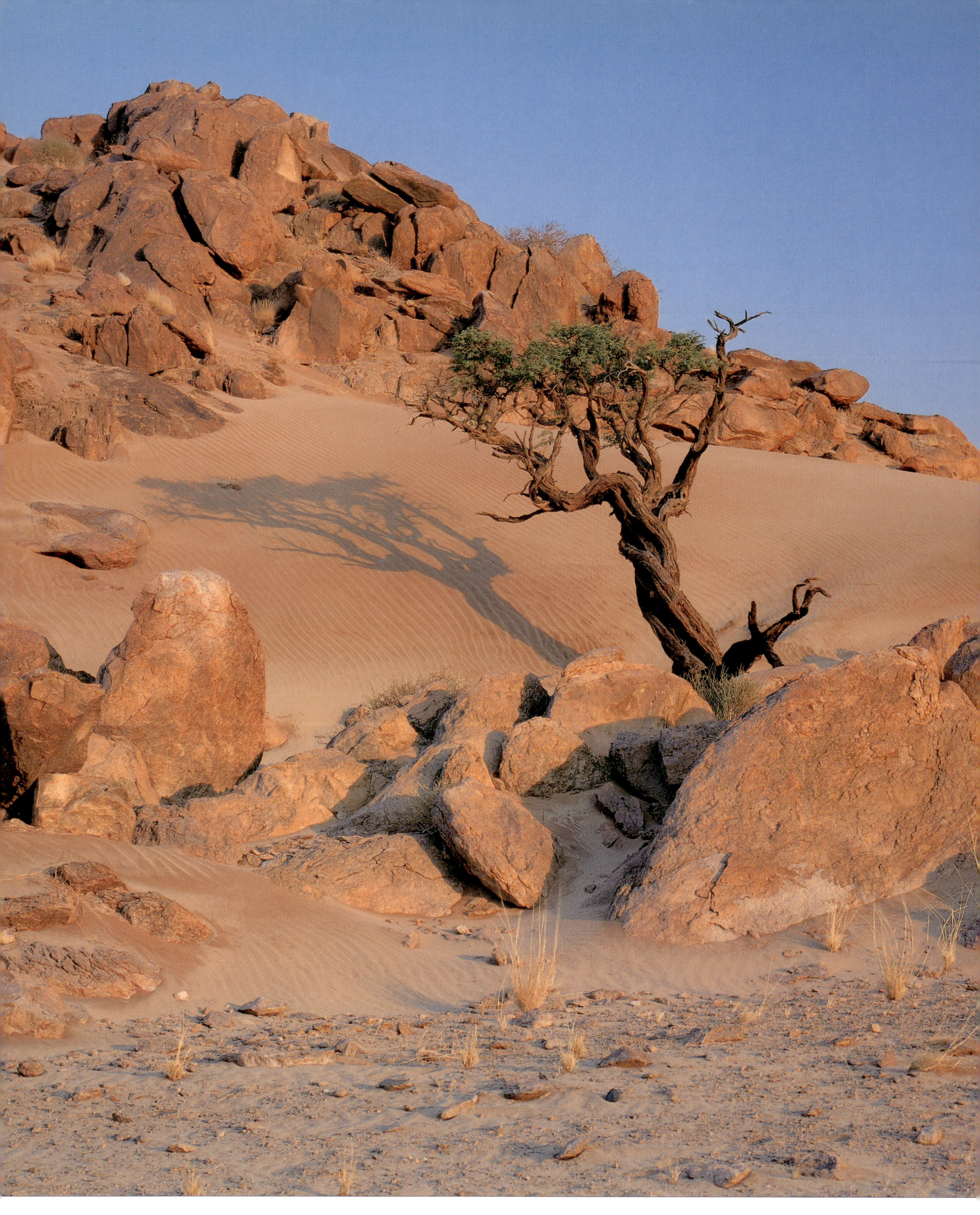

Photographic opportunities lie anywhere and everywhere across the Namibian landscape where even simple beauty explodes with spectacular colour, as in this rocky outcrop near Sesriem Canyon.

INTRODUCTION

Namibia is a country full of chart-topping natural wonders: the world's largest sand dunes; its largest intact meteorite; its oldest desert; and, reputedly, its largest elephants. Not far behind is the world's second largest canyon. No less impressive are such awesome spectacles as the vast Etosha salt pan that is the heart of Etosha National Park. This magnificent park, one of the largest game reserves in Southern Africa, is home to a breathtaking volume and variety of wildlife.

As you journey around Namibia, fascinating land formations are like an 'open book' on the country's geological history, a story which began many millions of years ago with the breakup of the Gondwanaland super-continent. Extinct volcanoes and dolerite dykes, fractured massifs and eroded plains, expansive deserts and parched riverbeds are all attributed to the tectonic and meteoric upheavals this land has endured throughout its evolution.

Across this remarkable landscape unique and intriguing vegetation continues the story of relentless struggle against remorseless climatic conditions - a story with many heroic endings. For example, the dense lichen fields that stretch endlessly across coastal sand dunes lie shrivelled and, seemingly, lifeless under the harsh sun, but spring into green abundance when the sea fog drifts in. Many of Namibia's amazing plants have adapted to the harsh environment and developed survival instincts that allow them to withstand the sparse, infrequent rainfall.

Namibia has a mystical effect on its visitors. It is partly a visual affair, partly esoteric. It stirs murmurings deep within, at times lifting the spirit to what can only be described as euphoria. The rich warm colours of the expansive, uncluttered landscape, the wildlife and the welcoming nature of its people captured my soul from my very first visit. To all those who live here and have made Namibia the wonderful place it is, I can only say thanks.

For those who have travelled these highways before, a toast to the magnet that pulls us back. To those who are visiting Namibia for the first time, welcome to this extraordinary land that will forever remain in your heart.

Rob Bickford

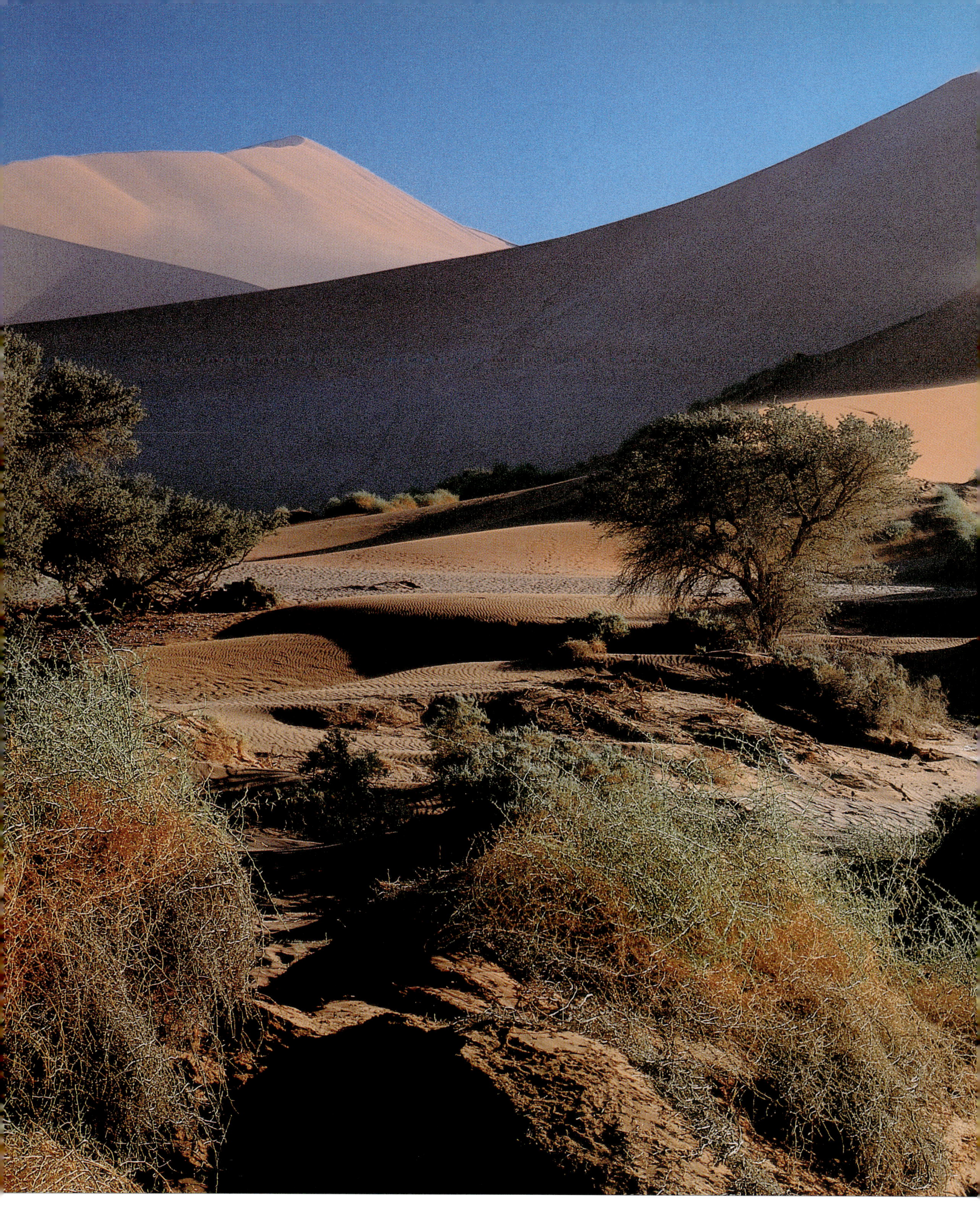

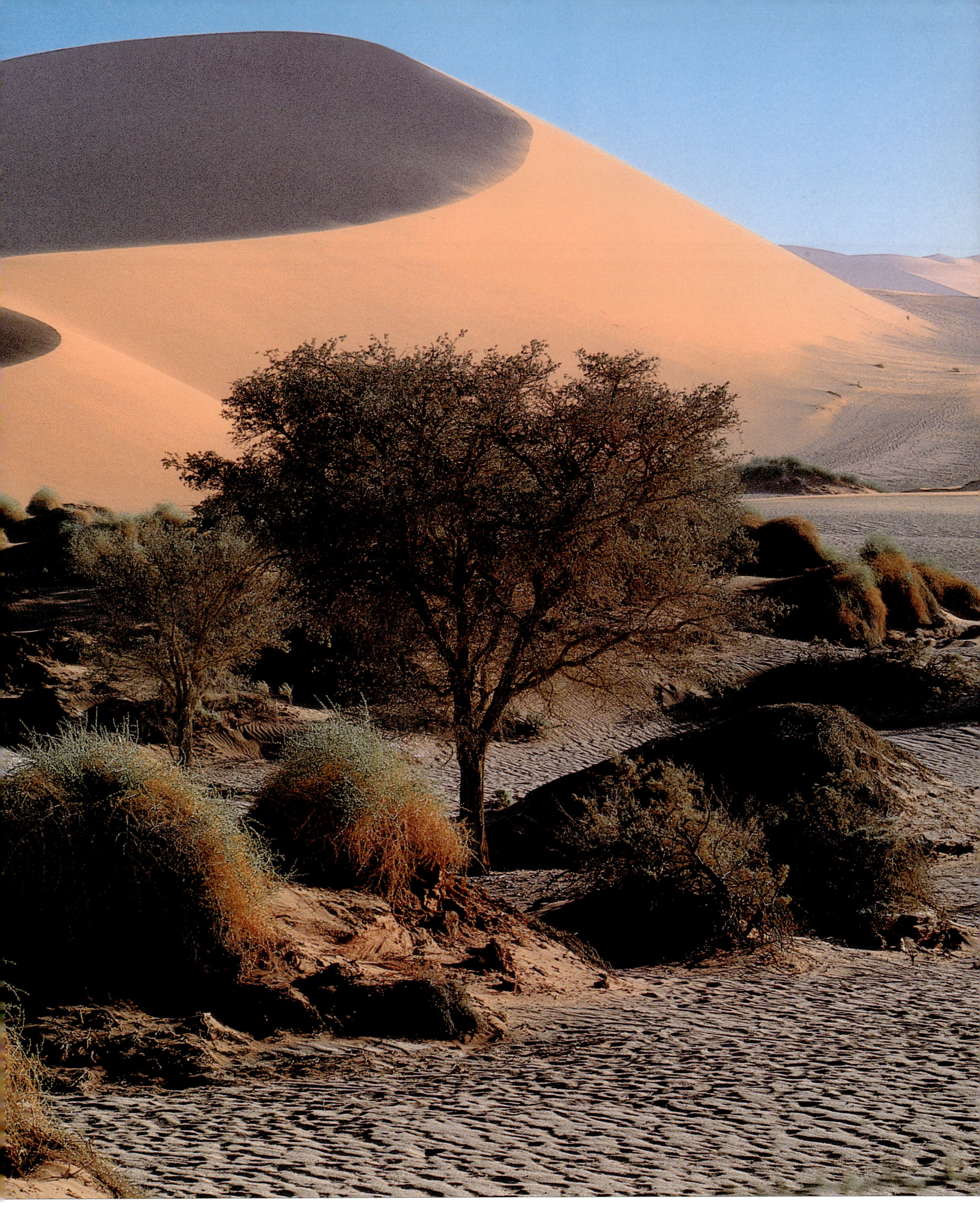

The drive from Sesriem to Sossusvlei is, in itself, spectacular but at the end of the road lies this magnificent dune, a drawcard for many photographers.

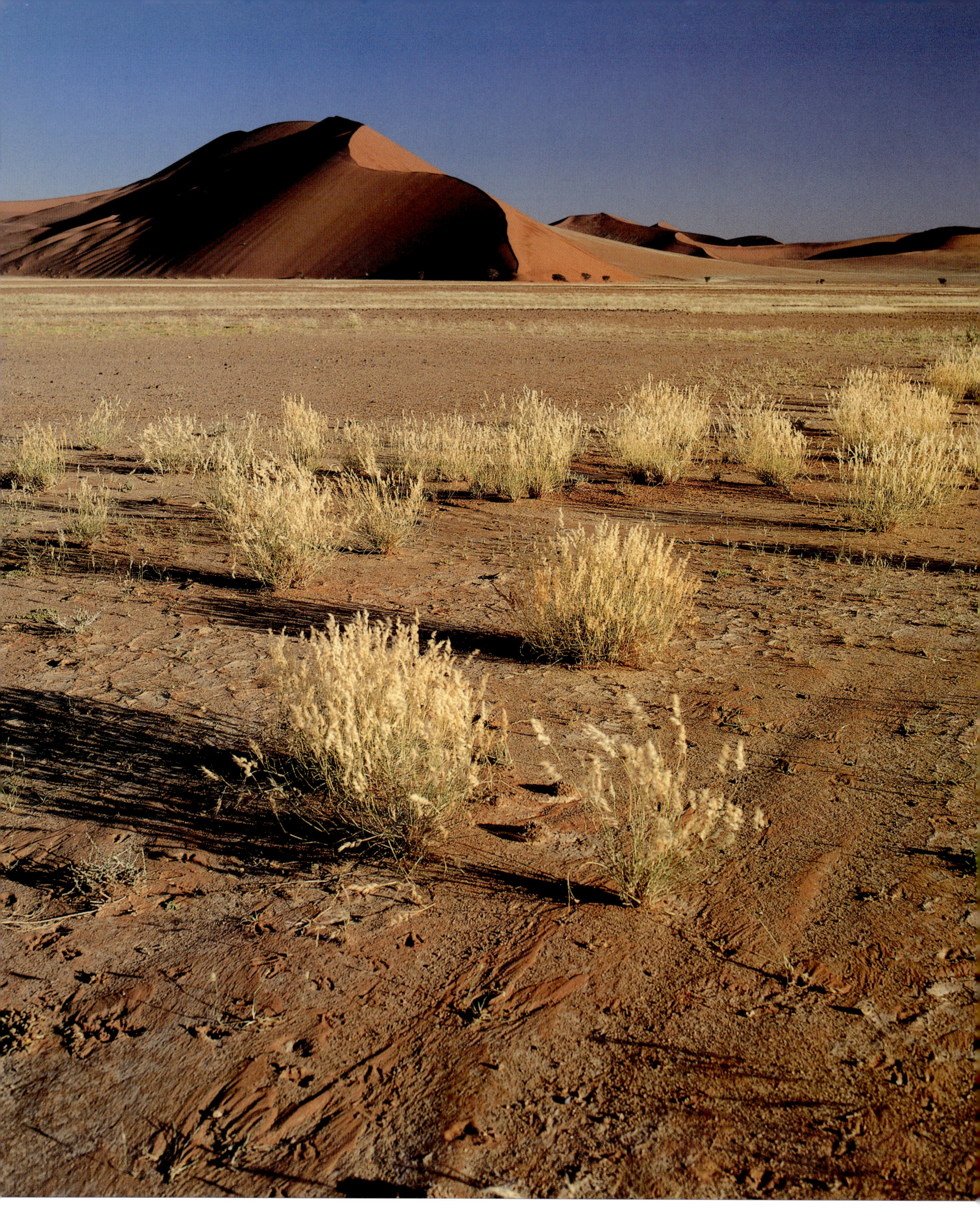

Just a sprinkling of rain prompts gentle grasses to sprout from the parched Tsauchab riverbed. Only a serious deluge restores the river to its full might.

SOSSUSVLEI - VALLEY OF DUNES

The Namib-Naukluft Park, covering an area of nearly 50,000 square kilometres, is one of the largest nature reserves on our planet. At Sossusvlei, in the park's southern reaches, drifting, mountainous sand dunes cloak the Namib Desert, the world's oldest desert, in grandeur and glory.

A road tracks the course of the dried-up Tsauchab riverbed from Sesriem through a valley of soaring sand peaks to reach the most famous of the dunes at Sossusvlei. Here, mighty ridges reaching 300 metres and higher encircle a parched greyish-white clay pan or vlei.

The wind dictates the contours of the dunes, constantly rearranging the razor-edged slopes and corrugated plains, while the sun plays artist with colours and shadows. Richly tinted flanks, from pale pink and apricot to vivid red and orange, make this a magical, moody landscape, particularly at sunrise when the colour transformation is most dramatic.

Known as star dunes because they are formed by equally strong winds from different directions, the Sossusvlei dunes are reputed to be the world's highest. In fact, they are not free-standing but rest on the 30-million-year-old Tsondab Sandstone terraces which are, themselves, the petrified remnants of a much older dune field from an ancient Namib. Thus, the landscape at Sossusvlei epitomises two distinct desert epochs separated by a long period during which a more humid climate reigned.

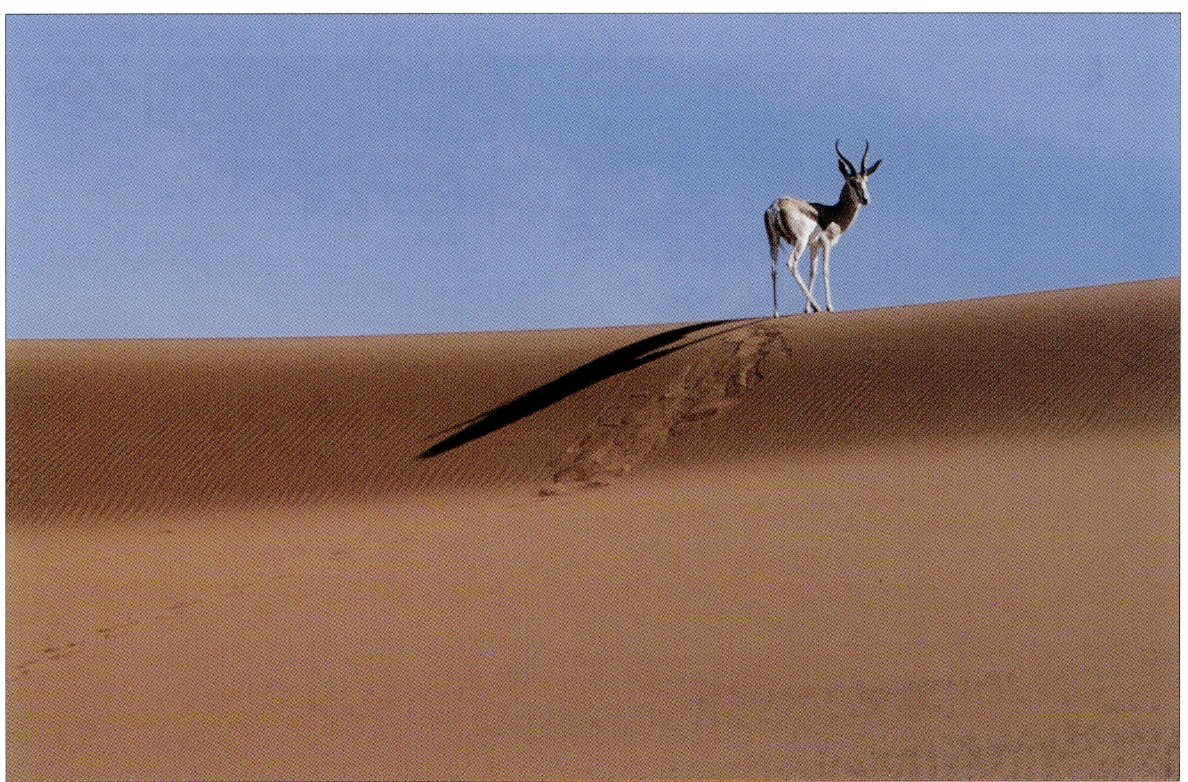

Springbok, ostrich and gemsbok (oryx) are often encountered roaming through Sossusvlei's inhospitable environs or ghosting phantom-like out of sandstorms that swirl through the valley.

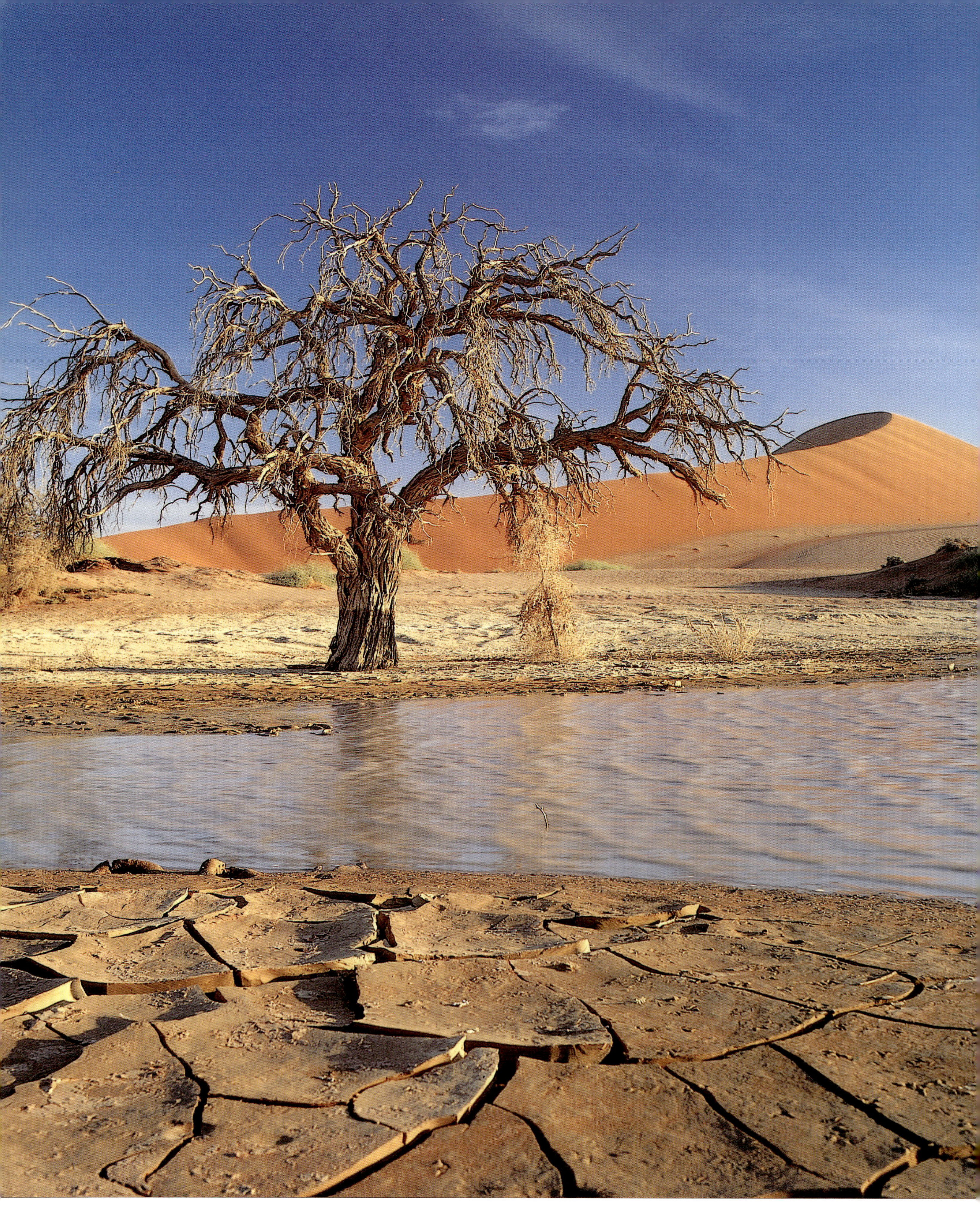

In February 1997, Sossusvlei was deluged with a once-in-30-years flood that left the landscape splattered with rippling lakes. When the sun returned these evaporated into lattice-like mud crusts.

SOSSUSVLEI - THE BIG RAINS

Skeletal camel thorns stand destitute on the Sossusvlei valley plains, stark illustrations of the incessant struggle endured by flora and fauna to survive in this drought-ridden and delicately balanced eco-system. Only every six or seven years does a major rainfall send the waters of the Tsauchab River raging through the Sesriem Canyon and down the valley toward the Atlantic as they did millions of years ago. But now the river dams up 50 kilometres short of the coast, cut off by the enormous dunes sitting in its path. The Sossusvlei fills with water, and rippling oases lend new splendour and perspective to this already magnificent landscape. The surrounding countryside explodes with life. Even the dune slopes sprout bushy shrubs and gentle, shimmering grasses.

Seeds of the Namib, able to withstand extremes of both heat and cold, can lie dormant for extraordinarily long periods of time. With a good drenching, even for just a few moments, many plants can flourish, flower and bear fruit within three weeks. Then, for a blink of time, the normally red, arid land erupts with a lavish display of indigenous plants and silvery-green grasses.

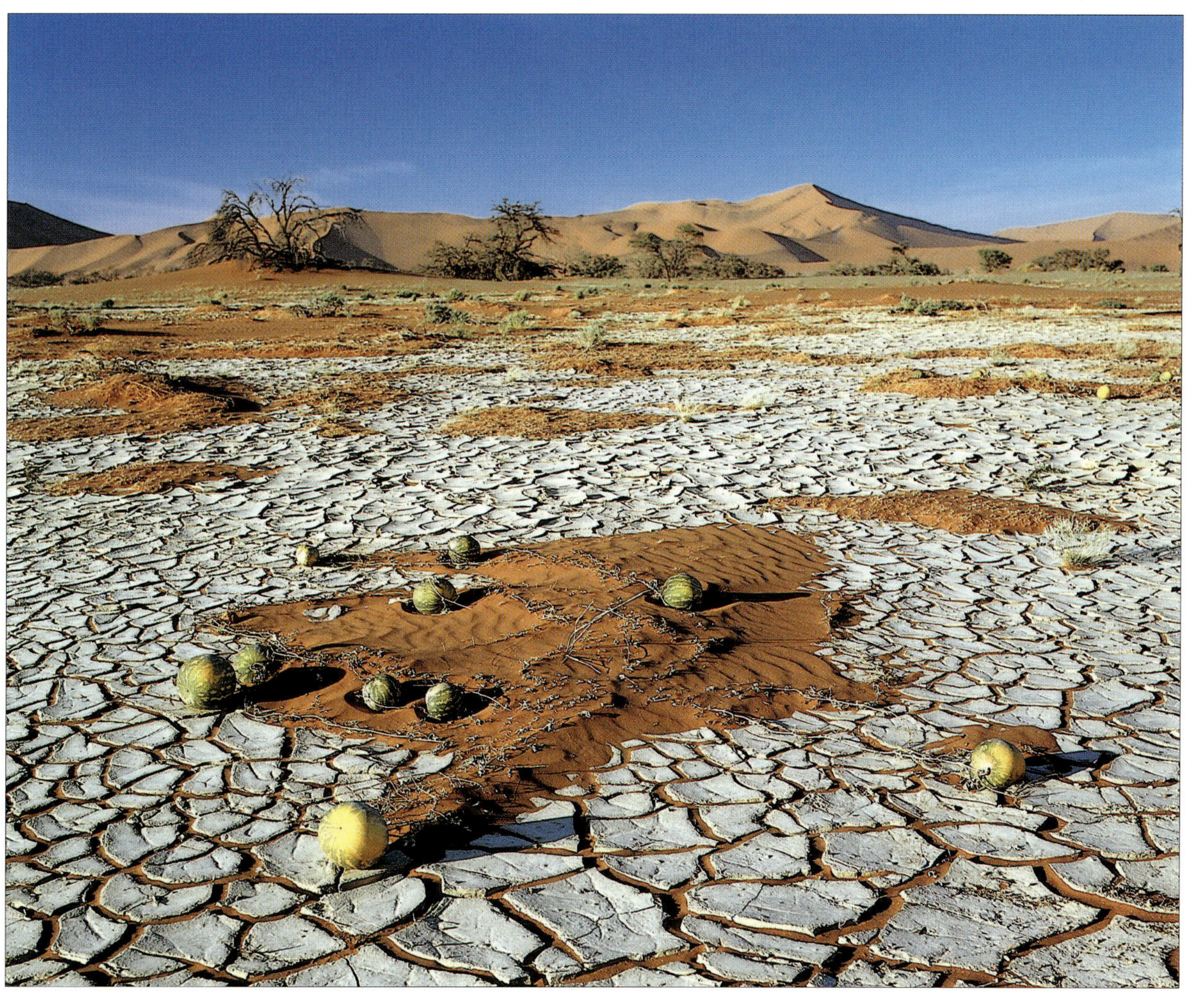

The fruit of the tsamma melon, like many other succulents sprinkled across the sandy landscape, provide critical moisture for many desert-dwelling animals.

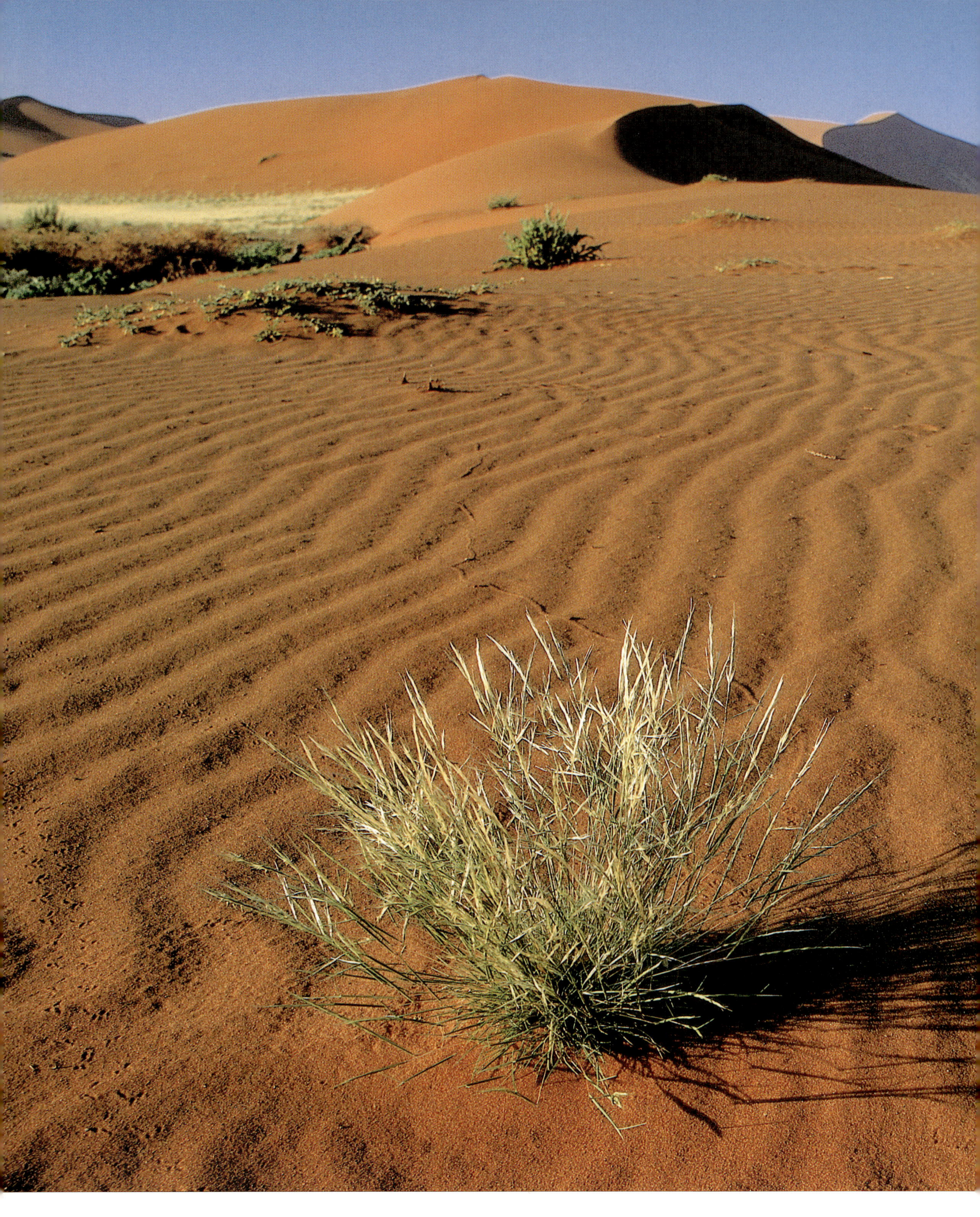

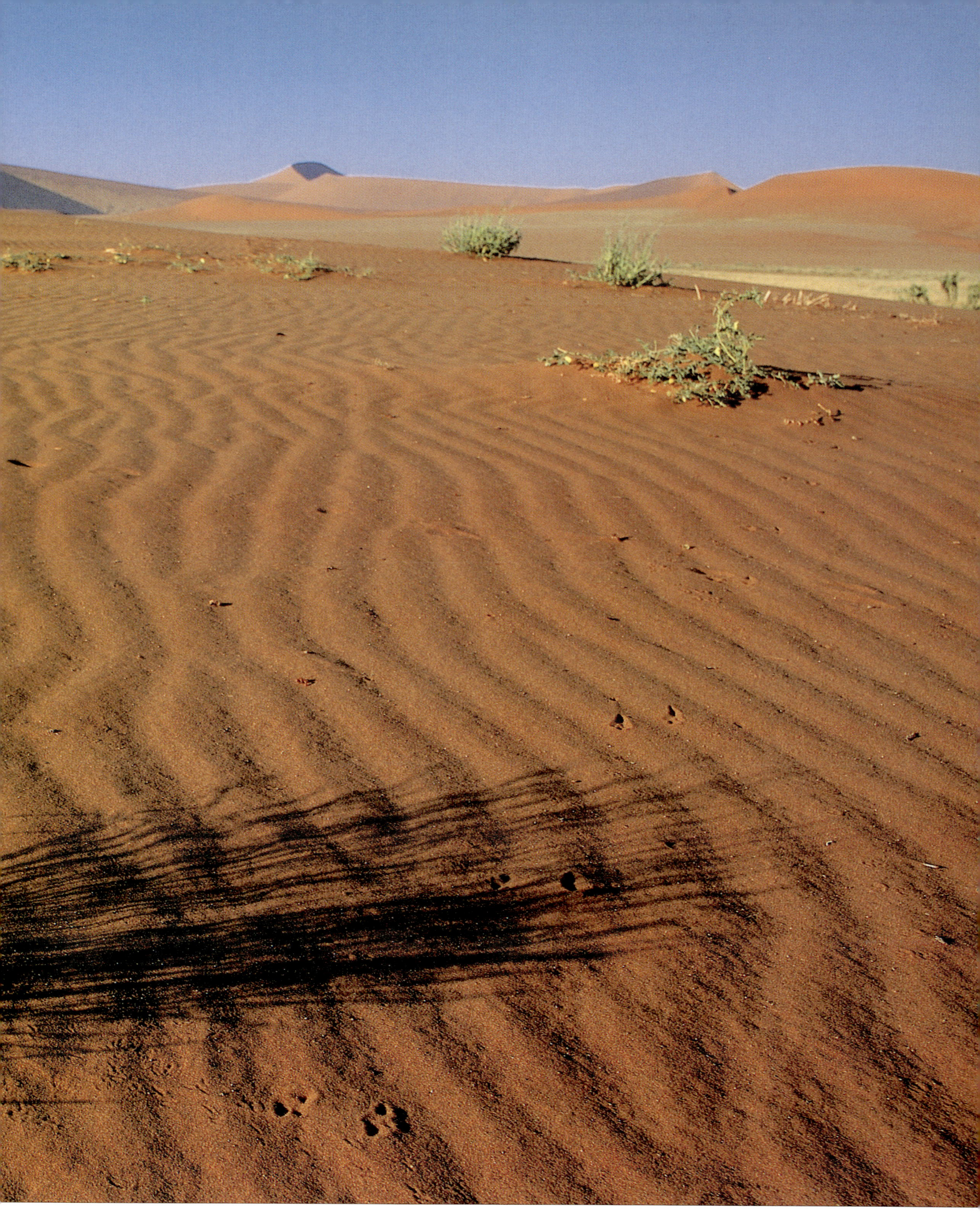

The barren, haunting expanse of the Namib-Naukluft National Park extends from the rugged Naukluft Mountains in the east, across the mighty Namib Desert, to the Atlantic Ocean.

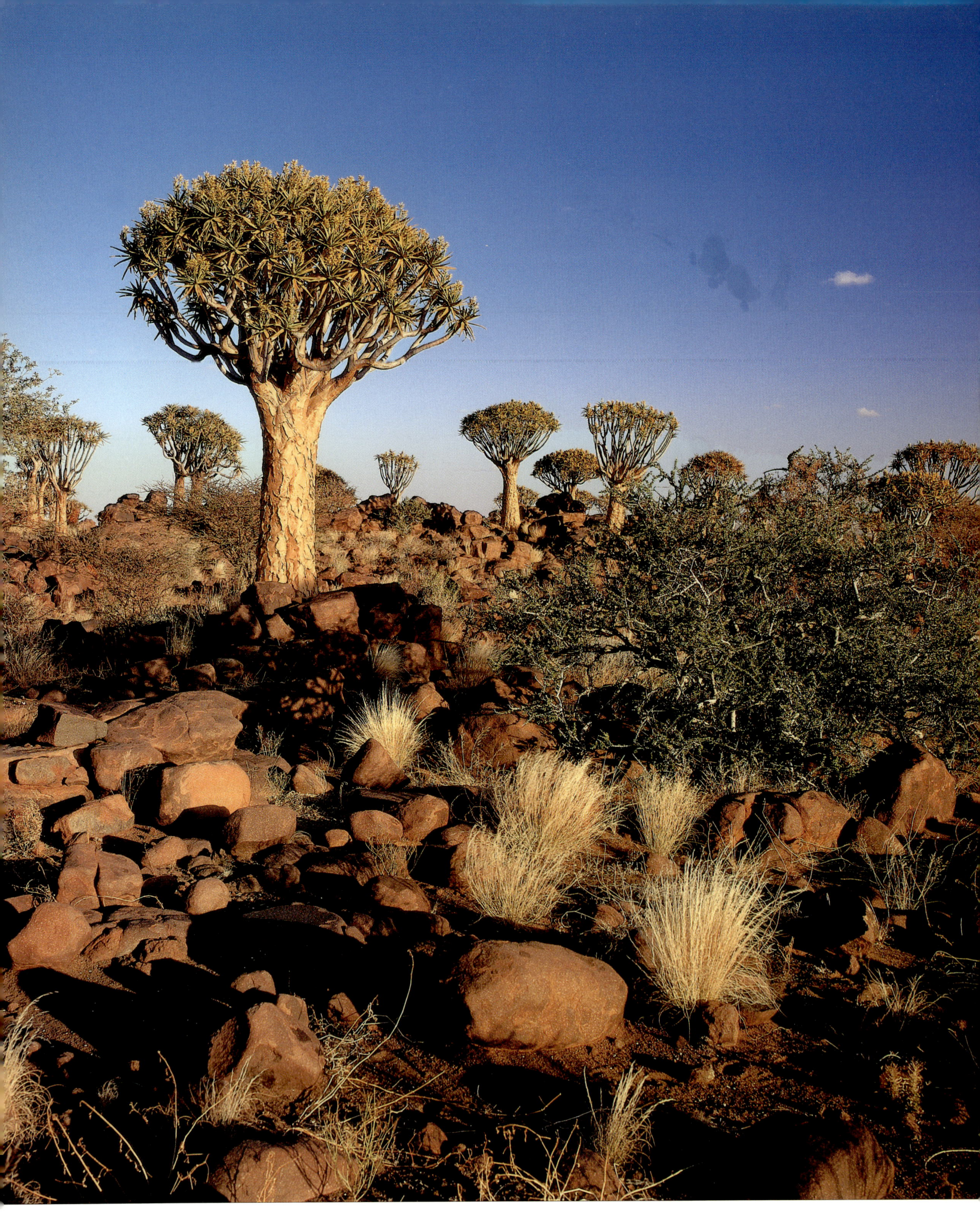

The kokerboom or quiver tree is restricted to the arid southern areas of Namibia. It is unusual to find such a dense stand as this, which occurs at the Quiver Tree Forest near Keetmanshoop.

THE QUIVER TREE FOREST

One of Namibia's most intriguing natural phenomena can be found on the Gariganus farm east of Keetmanshoop. Here around 300 quiver trees or kokerboom *(Aloe dichotoma)*, which usually grow in solitude, are forested together. These trees, some estimated at between 200-300 years old, are the world's largest aloe. They stand in spooky splendour amongst the volcanic outcrops that litter the rust-coloured hills.

The slow-growing kokerboom can reach up to nine metres with a diameter of up to one metre at the trunk base. Its fibrous trunk, slender branches and pithy leaves become water reservoirs, allowing the tree to withstand the harsh conditions of the parched, rocky wasteland in Namibia's western hardveld. In times gone by, the San bushmen used the hollowed-out branches as quivers for their arrows, giving the tree its common name.

The Gariganus farm also offers sanctuary to rogue or abandoned wildlife. Rescued wildlife residents thrive there, roaming footloose and fancy-free, yet with the luxury of always having food on the table.

Five kilometres down the road from the Quivertree Forest, on another corner of the farm, lies the Giant's Playground where precariously balanced rocks resemble toy building blocks put carefully in place by a young Goliath. These rocks were, in fact, exposed by the erosion of surrounding soft deposits.

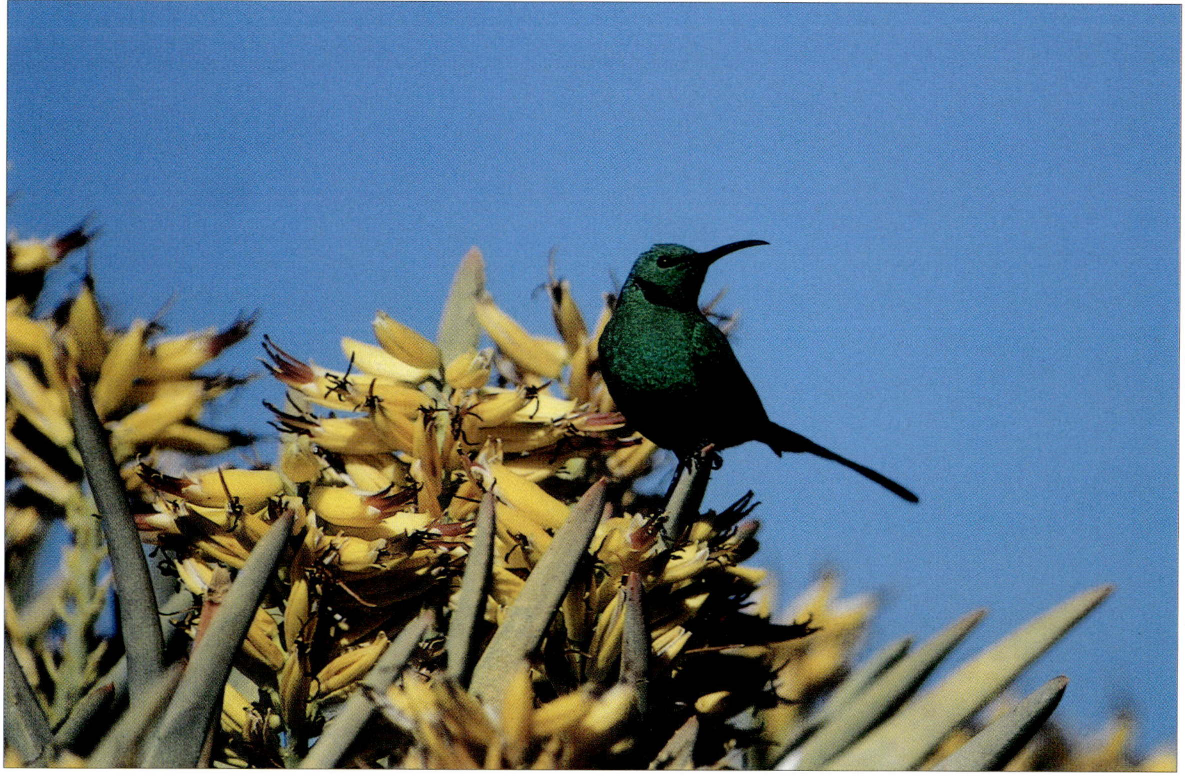

The crown of the quiver tree is a bright yellow mass of flowers when the aloe is in full bloom during June and July. A malachite sunbird alights on one of the nectar-laden flowers.

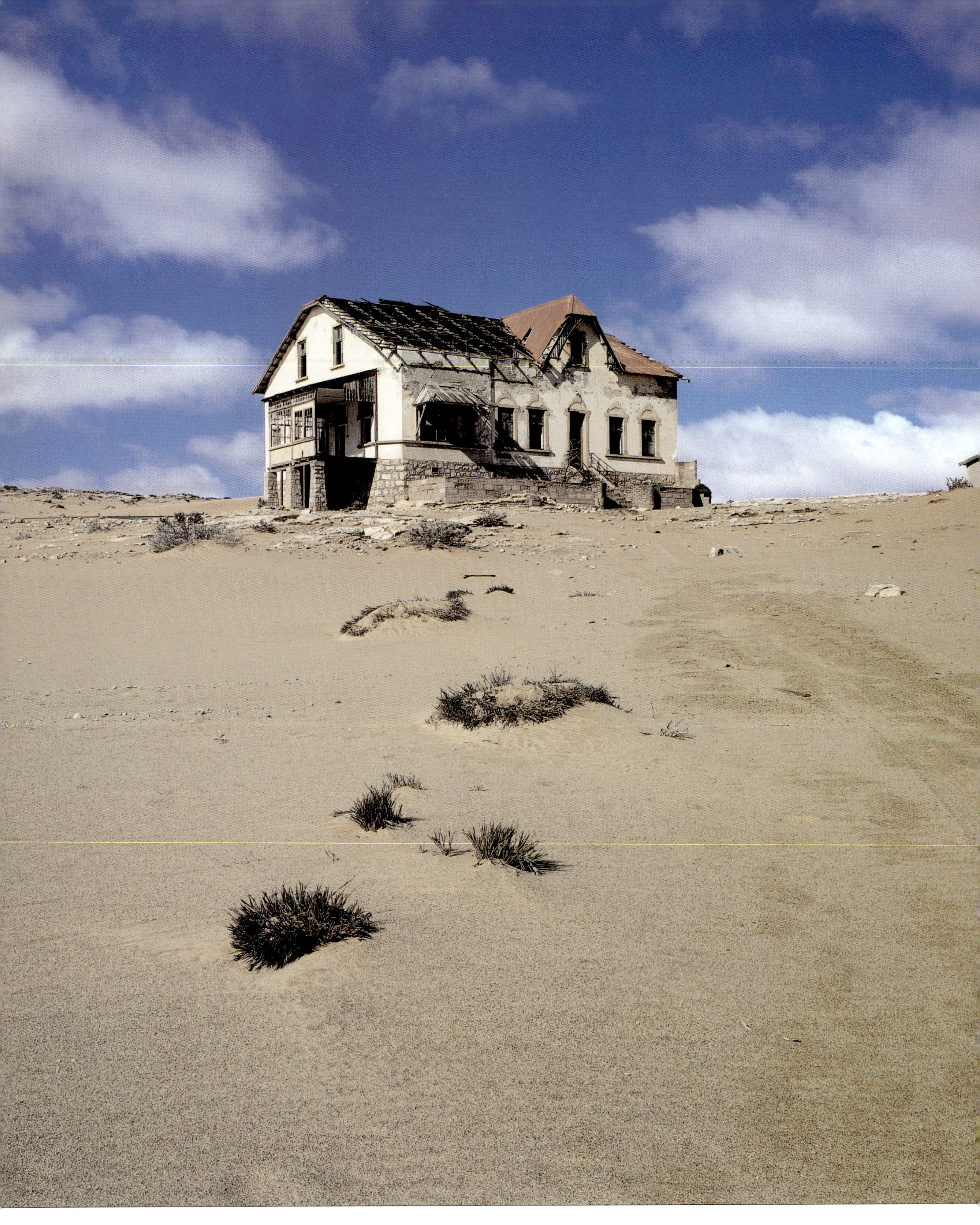

The abandoned town of Kolmanskop offers an irrestible peek into the intrigue, excitement and greed of a diamond rush of monumental proportions.

THE DIAMOND GHOSTS OF KOLMANSKOP

Ten kilometres inland from the Atlantic Ocean, the forlorn ruins of Kolmanskop lie strewn across the face of an unremarkable sand dune. When the wind blows it is easy to imagine the ghosts of lost dreams roaming restlessly through the ramshackle buildings of the buried town. For it was here that many a fortune was made and lost when diamond fever first gripped Namibia in the early 1900s.

Kolmanskop was named after the early Afrikaner trekker, Jani Kolman, whose ox wagon fell foul of a sandstorm there. Despite such inauspicious beginnings, the spot become a mecca for diamond miners when, in April 1908, railway worker Zacharias Lewala uncovered a pretty stone near Grasplatz, an insignificant train station dotted down in the desert between inland Keetmanshoop and coastal Lüderitz. Zacharias handed the interesting find to his supervisor, the astute Herr Stauch, who wasted no time taking out a prospector's licence. And so a diamond rush began. Such was the supply of the precious gems that pretty soon people were literally picking them off the ground. A settlement sprouted at Kolmanskop, a few kilometres to the west of Grasplatz, and grand residences rose from the sand to house miners lured there by tales of the fabulous wealth just waiting to be scratched from the desert. The German government soon proclaimed a Sperrgebeit or "forbidden territory", restricting mining to mining companies. Over five million carats - around a tonne – of diamonds were extracted at Kolmanskop between 1911 and 1914.

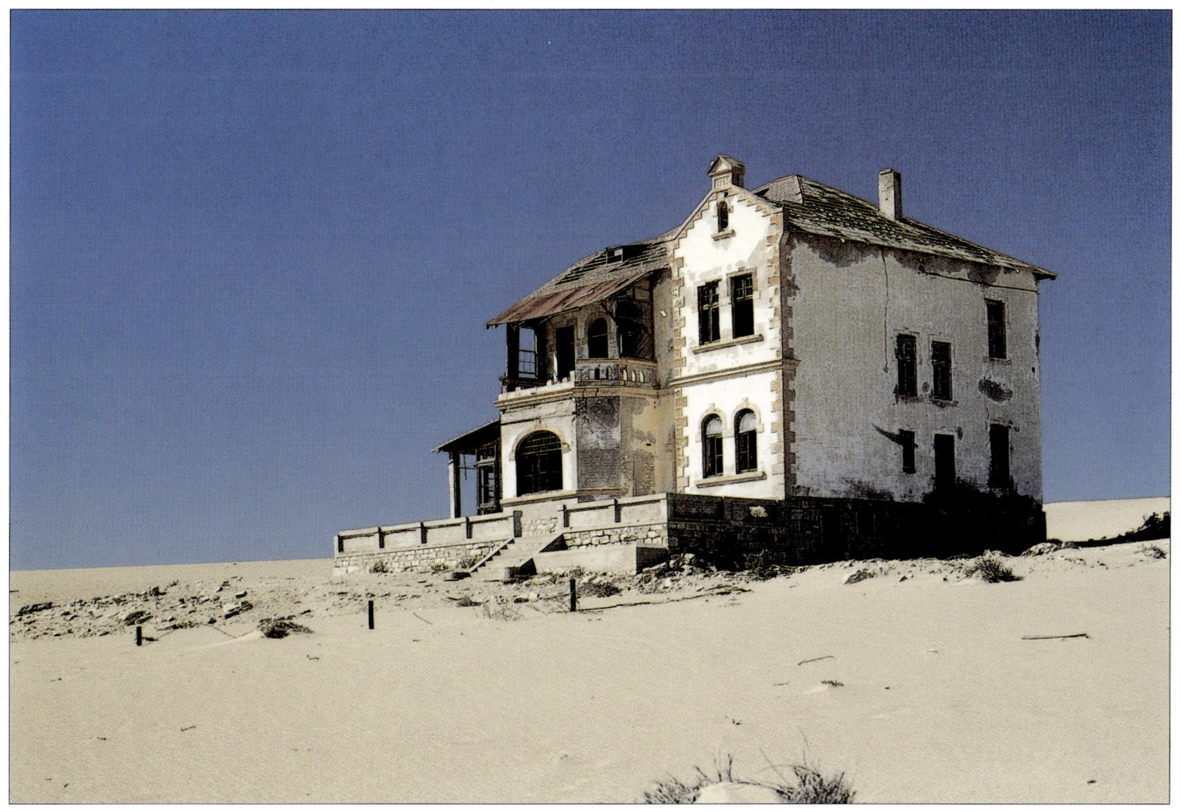

This formerly elegant mansion hints at the extravagant lifestyle enjoyed by mine management during Kolmanskop's heyday in the early 1900s.

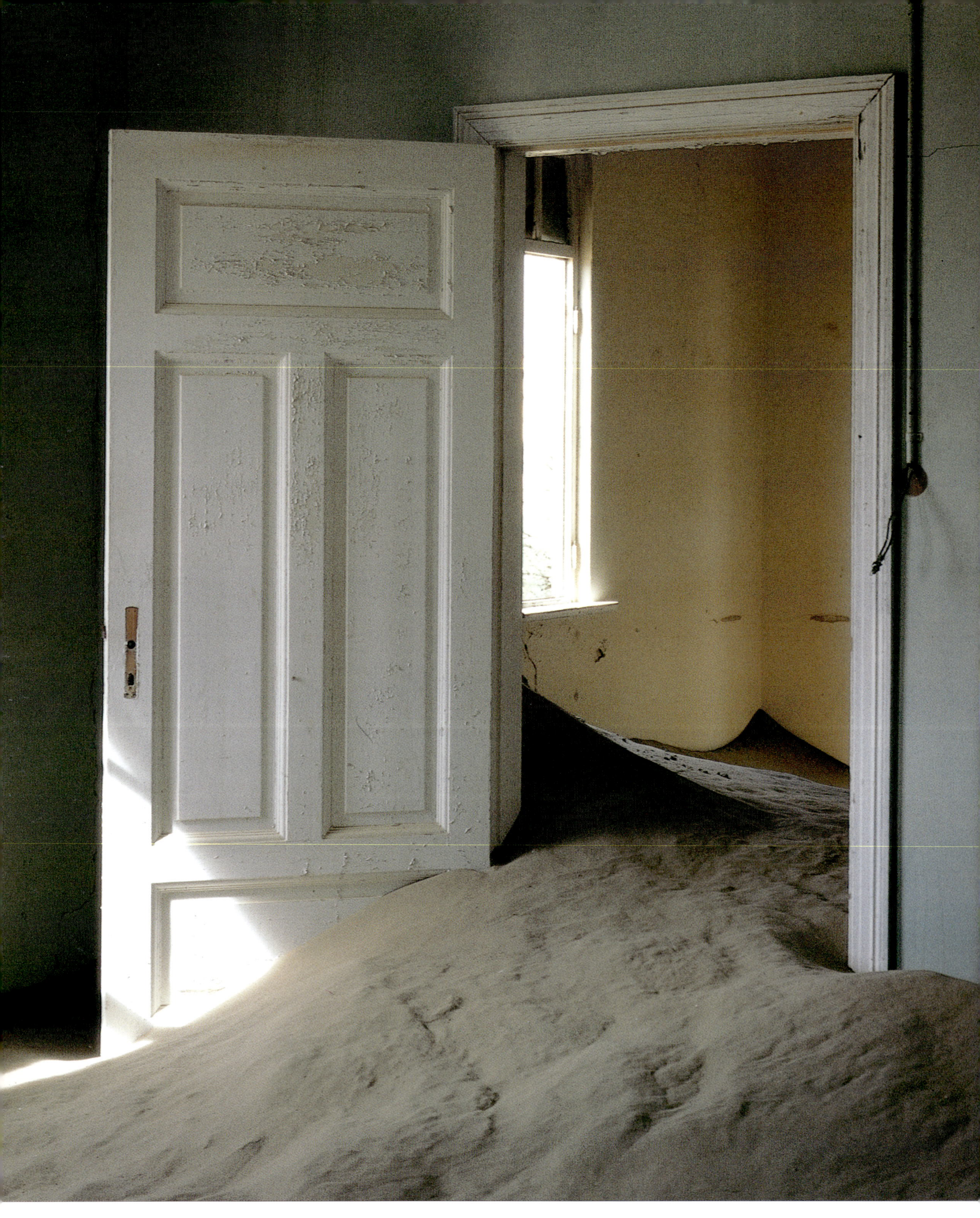

The desert winds continue to lash Kolmanskop's buildings. Once they've breached exterior defences, particles of sand burst through any openings and claim the interiors.

KOLMANSKOP - THE ABANDONED TOWN

In its glory days, Kolmanskop was the epitome of European elegance and the mine manager, along with other key personnel, lived the high life. Streets lined with grand residences, a casino, theatre, shop and school all sprang up out of the desert. The town's large and modern hospital was the first in Southern Africa to have an x-ray machine.

Services were established and a power station was built at nearby Lüderitz to generate electricity for the town and mining operation. At the height of diamond fever, Kolmanskop was home to more than 300 German prospectors and their children, as well as 800 Ovambo labourers from the north. Abundant riches afforded the miners a lavish lifestyle for around a decade before Kolmanskop's fortunes began to wane.

The town may have had its diamonds but it lacked essential natural resources, such as water, and was at the constant mercy of the ruthless, sandblasting winds. Fresh water was delivered from Capetown and, despite the harsh environment, mining continued there until 1938. However, dwindling diamond deposits coupled with richer finds to the south, spelt the end of the line for Kolmanskop. The town was finally left to the whim of the elements when the last resident departed in 1956, and the desert began to repossess the landscape.

Now almost completely submerged by the creeping sands of the Namib, the abandoned town offers an irresistible peek into the intrigue, excitement and greed of the times. Wind howls through lonely hallways and empty rooms, depositing sand in every abandoned nook and cranny. Sand piled high along deserted passageways and under empty window-frames both tempts and taunts, offering a constant reminder of the bewitching power of diamonds.

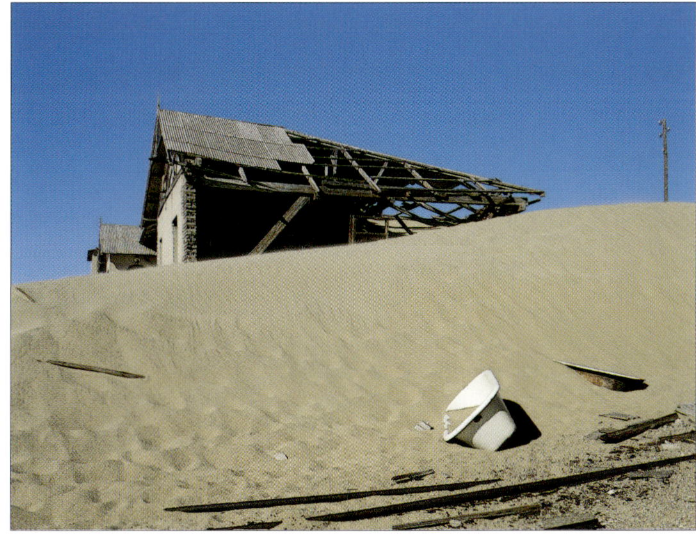

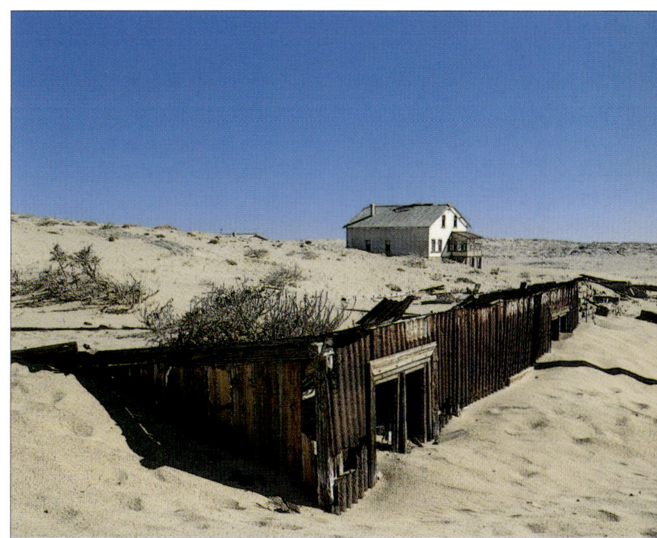

When the last inhabitants left the town in 1956 the Namib took its revenge, burying buildings up to their roofs and all but obliterating the evidence of a once thriving community.

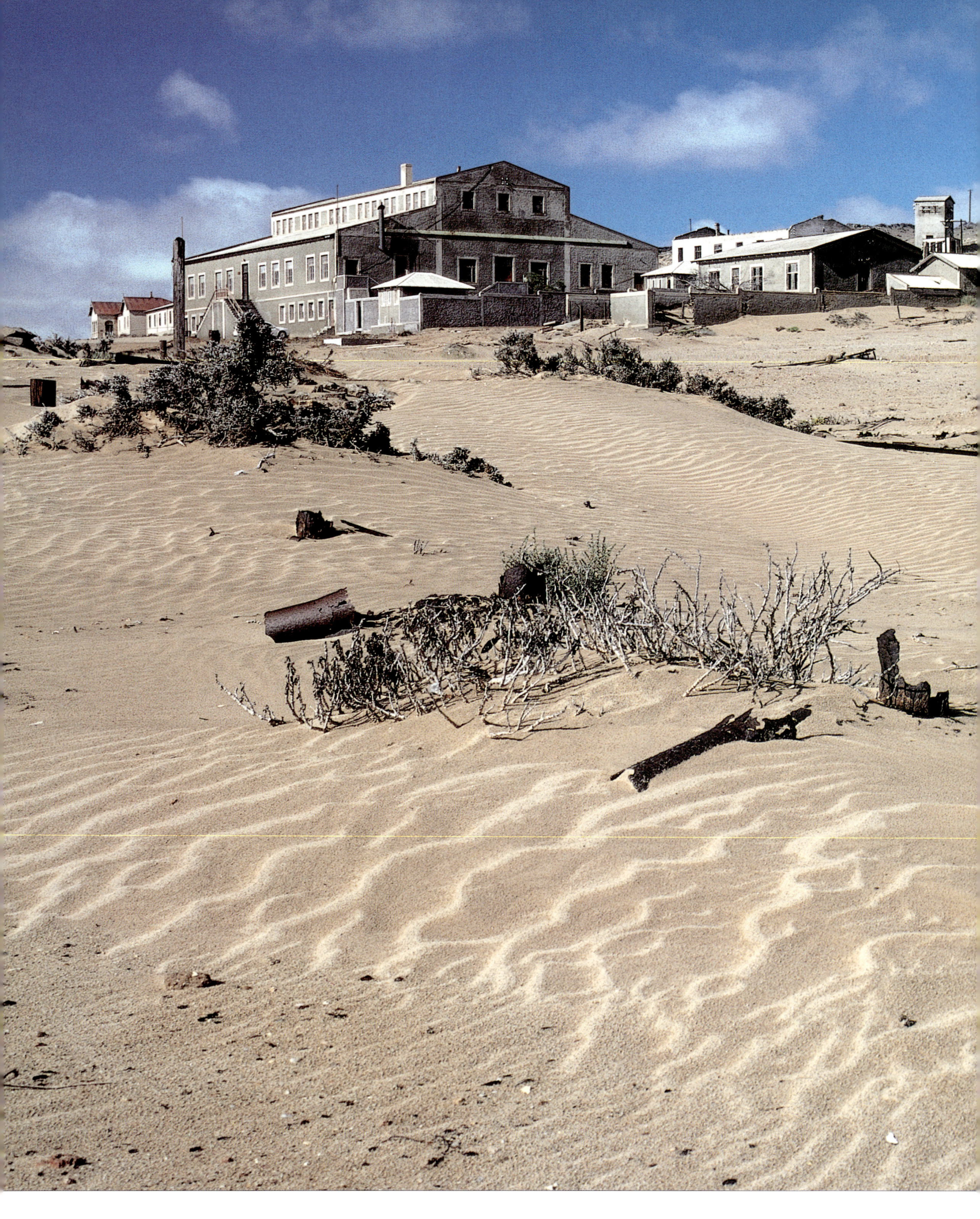

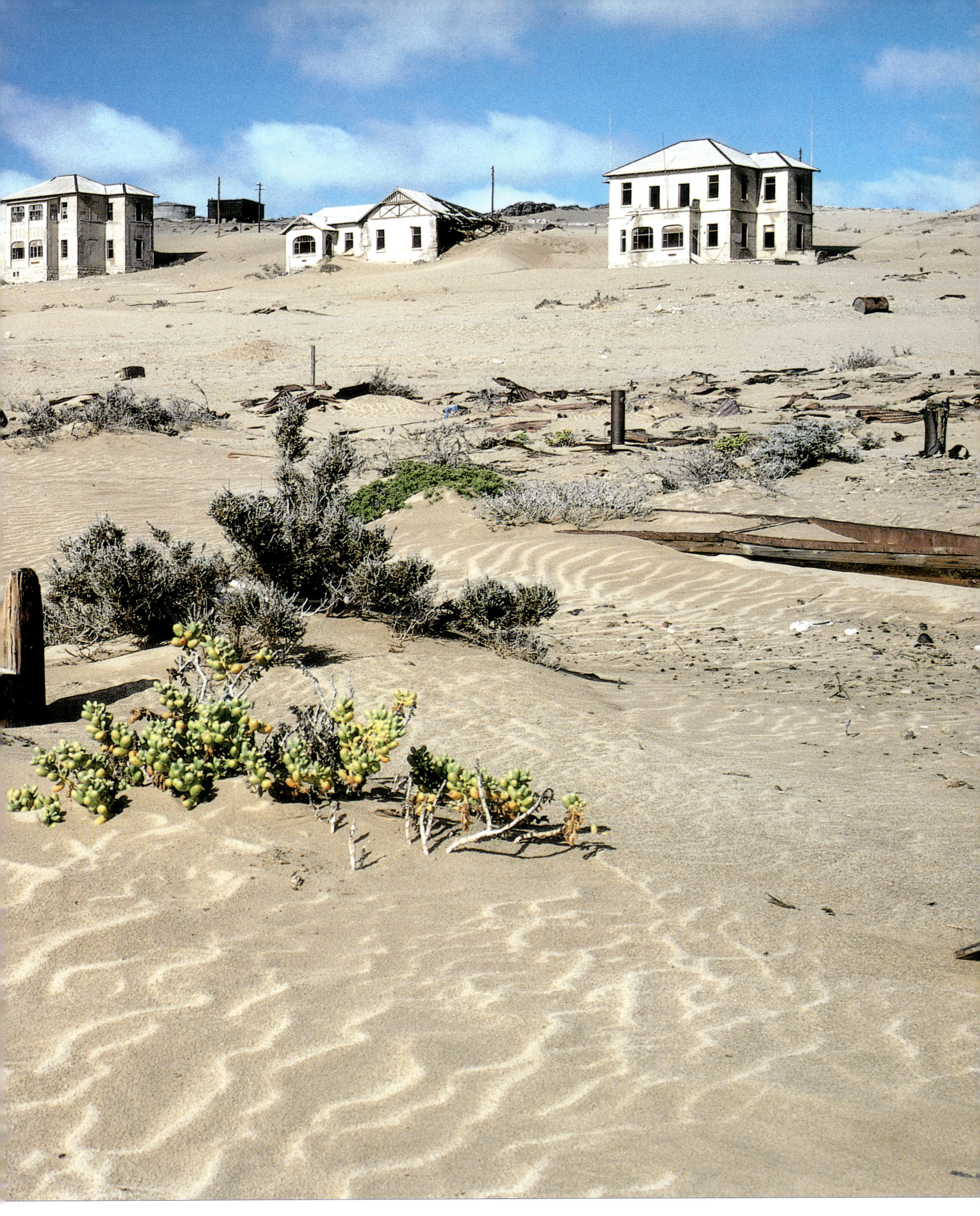

Ten kilometres inland from Lüderitz, Kolmanskop is an imposing graveyard of crumbling buildings that stand like headstones in honour of their own former magnificence.

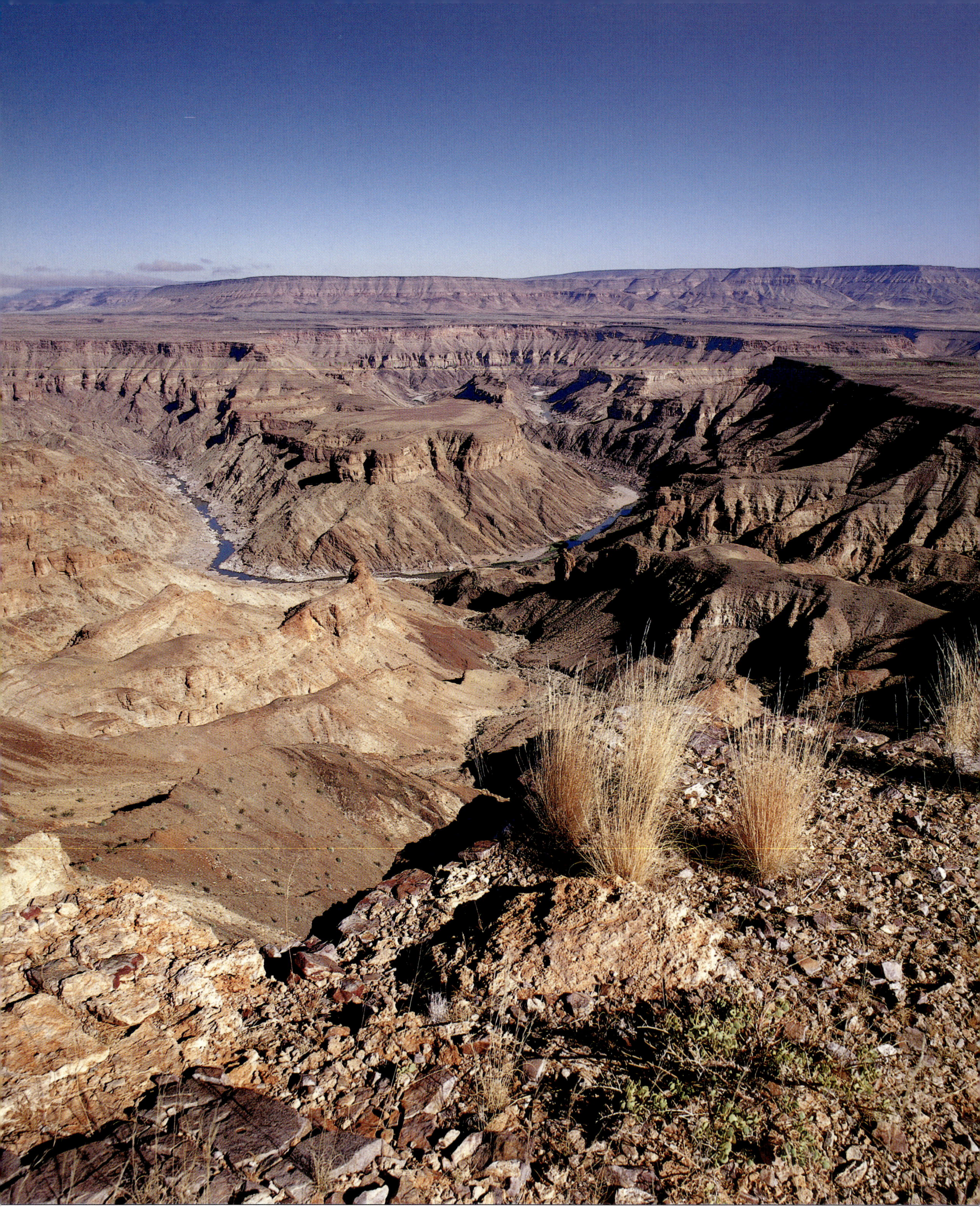

The Fish River Canyon, stretching to 27 kilometres at its widest and plunging to 549 metres at its deepest, winds through 161 kilometres of craggy, precipitous walls.

FISH RIVER CANYON

There is only one other canyon in the world to match the magnificence of Fish River Canyon. Although the canyon is smaller in size than North America's mighty Grand Canyon it is, nonetheless, a breathtaking spectacle. It was created by tectonic turmoil over countless millennia and further carved out by the raging torrents of the Fish River.

The canyon began forming about 350 million years ago. Layers of rock slid downwards along an adjacent ancient fault plain to form the original broad basin of the Fish River. The extremely hard quartzite rock of the basin floor prevented the Fish River from cutting deeply through deposits. Instead it was forced to ooze sideways, levelling out a plain known as the Hums Plateau. As the ancient river flowed across the plateau it chiselled out the gracious, sweeping meanders visible today. A few million years later, the breakup of Gondwanaland forced parts of Namibia to uplift. This increased the gradient and, therefore, the velocity of the Fish River, which caused it to cut deeper into the river loops and gnaw at the riverbed quartzite. Eventually, it reached the deepest layers of Namibia's most ancient rocks, seen today in outcrops at the bottom of the canyon.

The Fish River starts out in the Namib-Naukluft mountains to the north and journeys several hundred kilometres before tumbling over two waterfalls into the canyon. It is the exception among Namibia's rivers in that it retains perennial pools outside the rainy season. This makes the canyon a more accommodating habitat for wildlife. The nimble, rock-climbing klipspringer is a common inhabitant, as are kudu, Hartmanns mountain zebra, rock dassie (hyrax), ground squirrel and baboon. Leopard stalk and ostrich strut through the gullies of the canyon where birdlife is also plentiful.

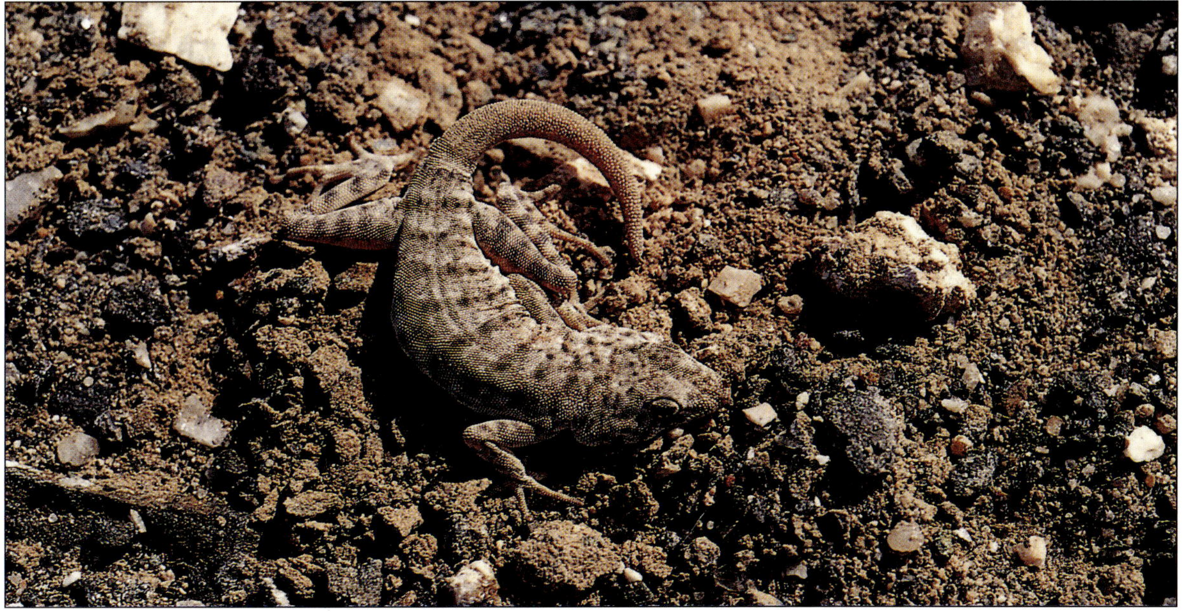

Like many reptiles that have adapted to the unforgiving, desert-like conditions that prevail across much of the country, this lizard's survival depends on its ability to remain invisible to predators.

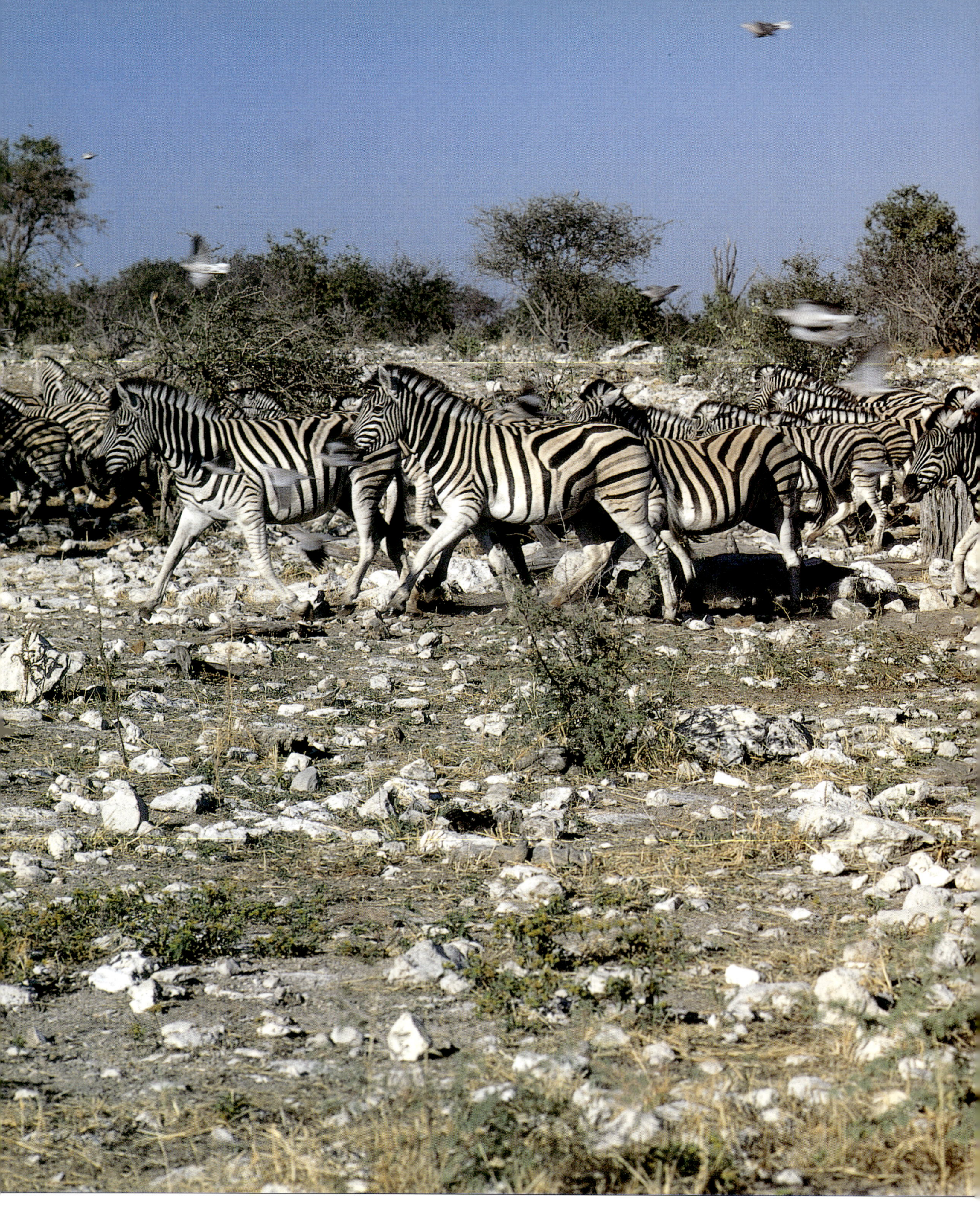

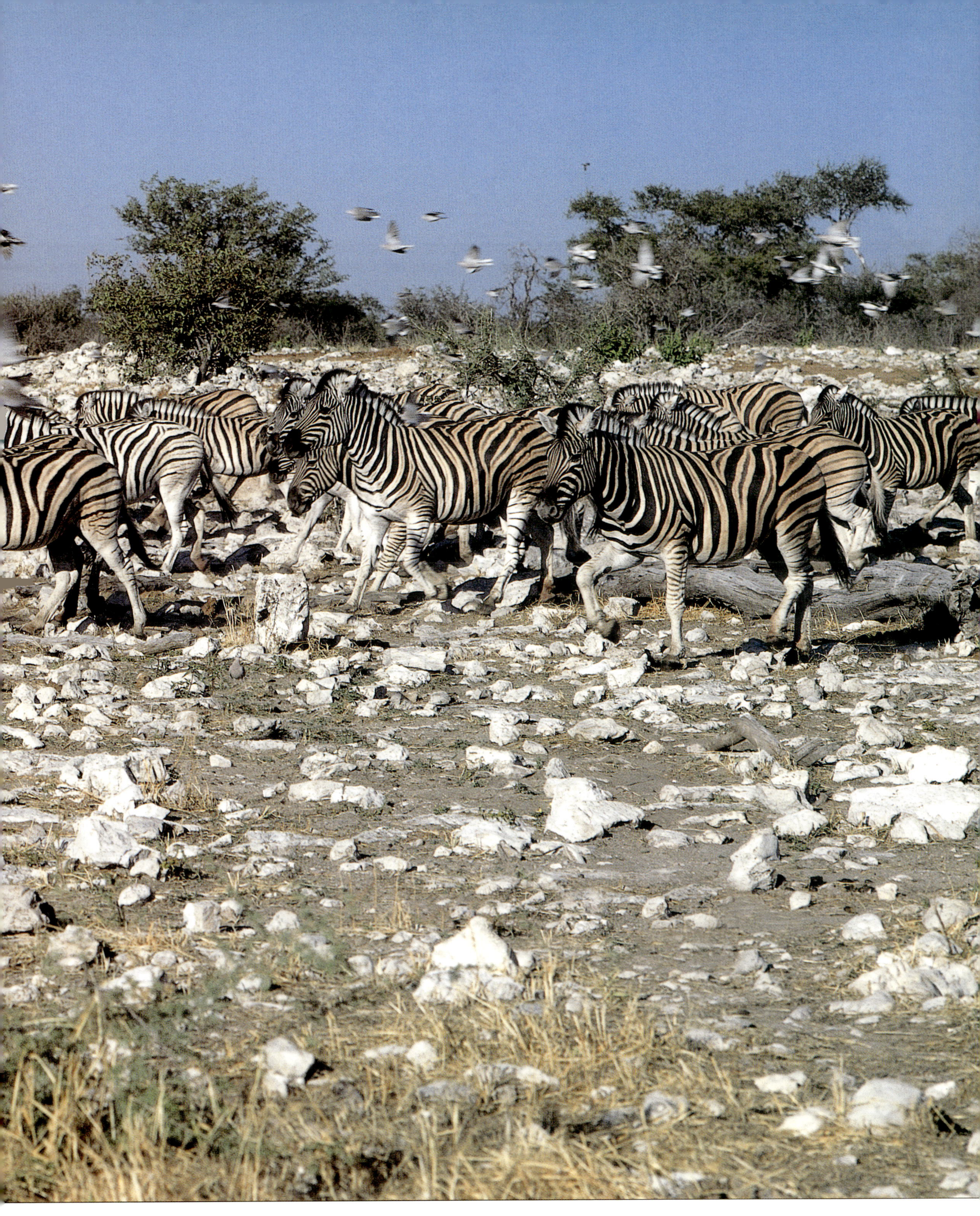

Namibia hosts an impressive volume and variety of wildlife. These Burchell's zebra, recognised by their shadow stripes, are suddenly 'spooked' at Kalkheuwel waterhole, Etosha.

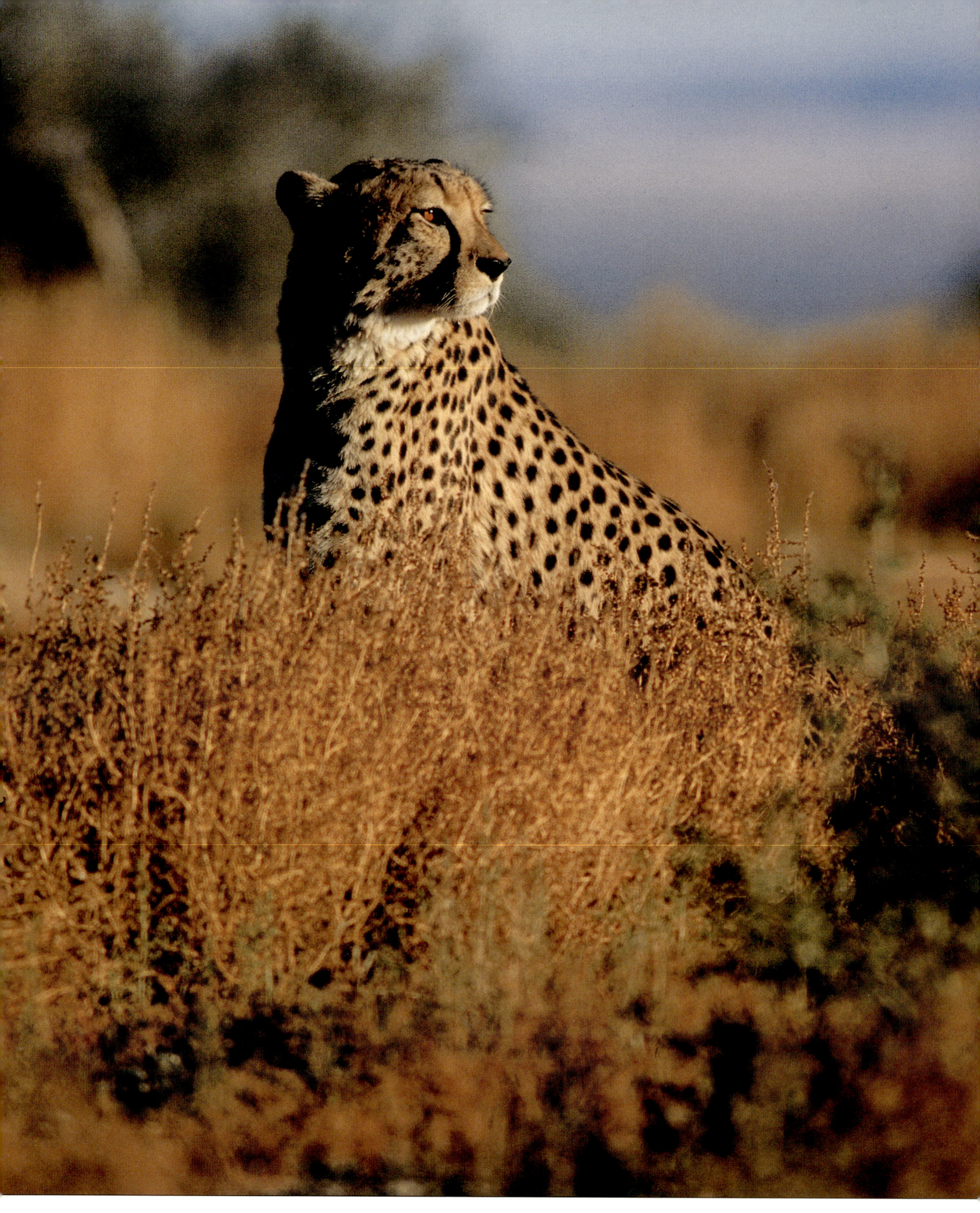

Namibia is renowned for its conservation of the highly-endangered cheetah. It is home to approximately 25 percent of the world's cheetah population.

WILDLIFE ENCOUNTERS

Wildlife enthusiasts need look no further than Namibia for spectacular game-viewing and close-up encounters of the most memorable kind. With around 15 percent of the country designated as national parks, most African game, including rare and endangered species, can be found here. Despite the ample accommodation provided for them, the largely semi-arid habitat poses unique challenges for resident wildlife and only the strongest individuals and species survive. Many common mammals such as gemsbok, springbok and elephant have become comfortable desert dwellers and can often be found travelling purposefully through the middle of what seems to be 'absolutely nowhere'.

Some of the finest viewing opportunities are found in Etosha National Park where action is usually just around the corner and the wildlife are generally obliging photographic subjects. Posers are plentiful, often appearing on cue and frequently in great numbers. The dry winter months are the most rewarding as animals drift from the waterless woodlands and plains to the many drinking holes dotted along the tourist route. Carnivores, herbivores, browsers and grazers, predators, scavengers, groupies and loners – they're all there.

Whether roaming protected in parks or free-and-easy in the wilderness, Namibia's wild animals bring unparalleled presence to the landscape.

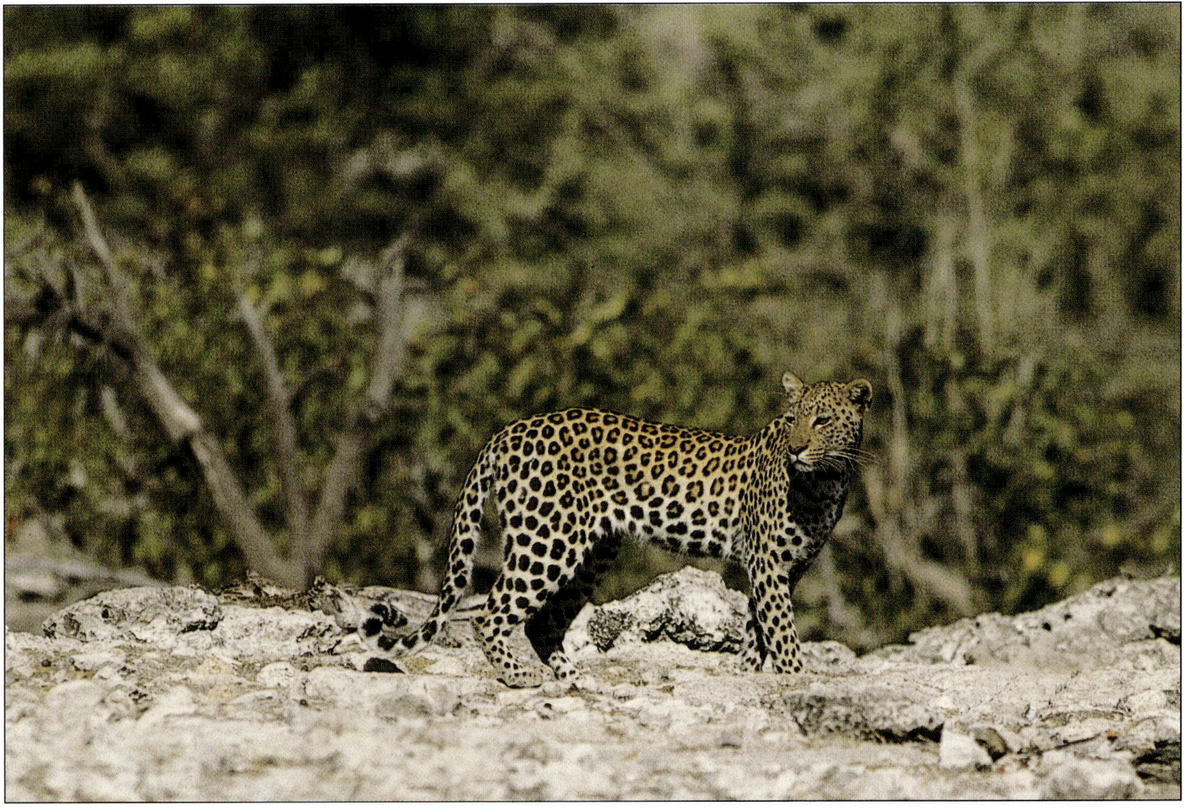

It is a special thrill when a leopard takes centre-stage as these shy, generally nocturnal cats like to avoid the limelight. This visitor lingered at Goas waterhole, Etosha, for just a few minutes.

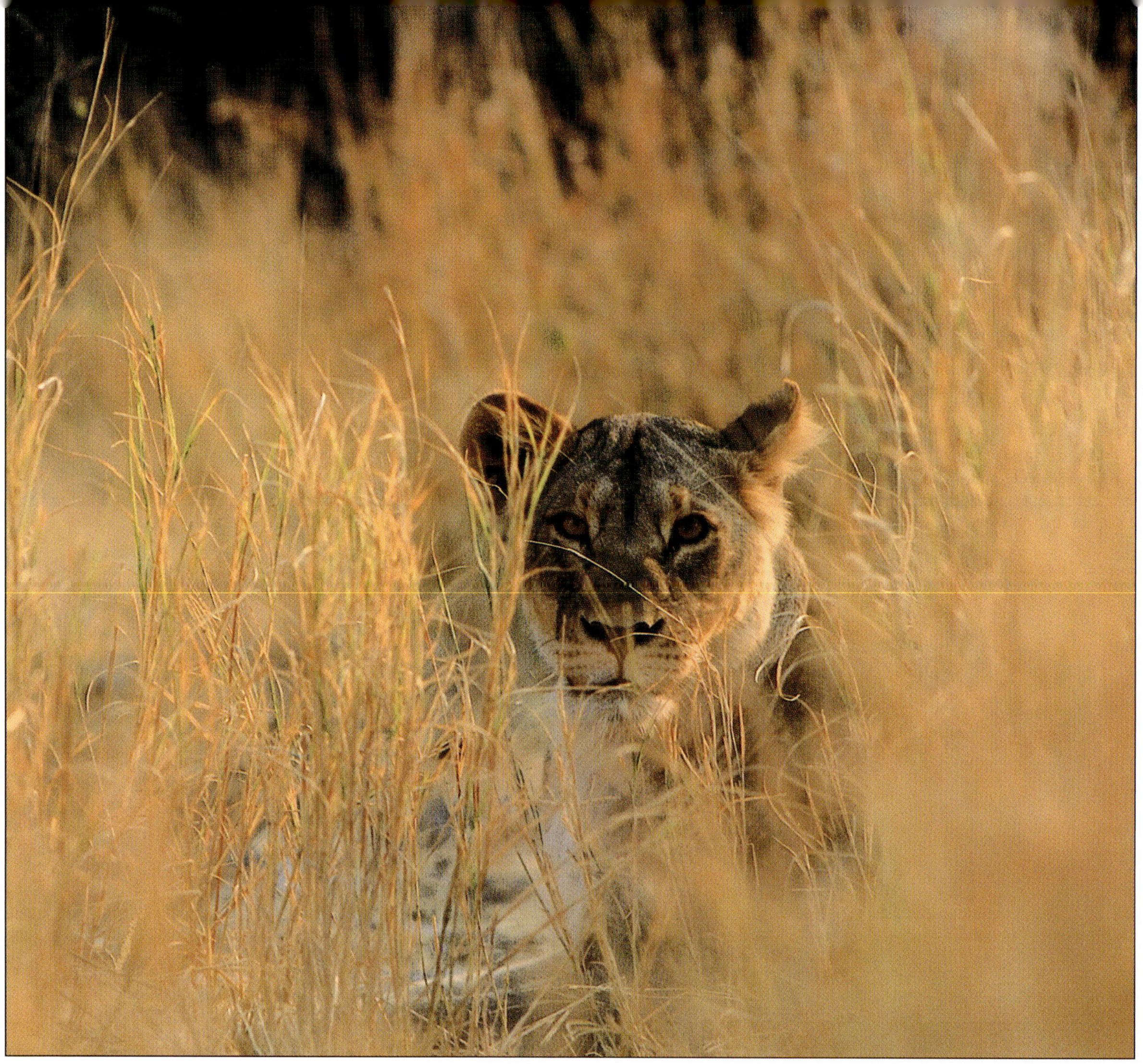

Blending tone-on-tone with the surrounding grasses, this ever-vigilant lioness is ready to pounce on any hapless herbivore careless enough to wander within her strike range.

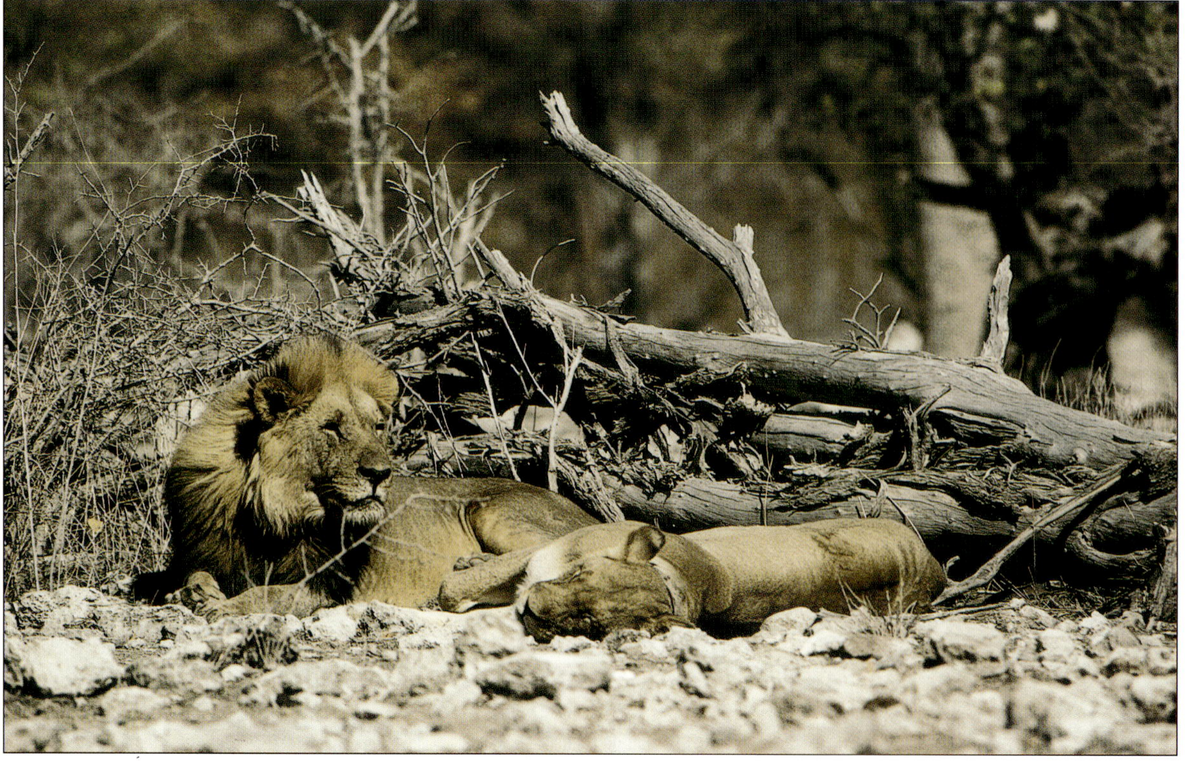

A pair of languid lions whiles away the heat of the day. Closer inspection reveals the lioness to be wearing a tracking collar to assist Etosha's conservation and research programmes.

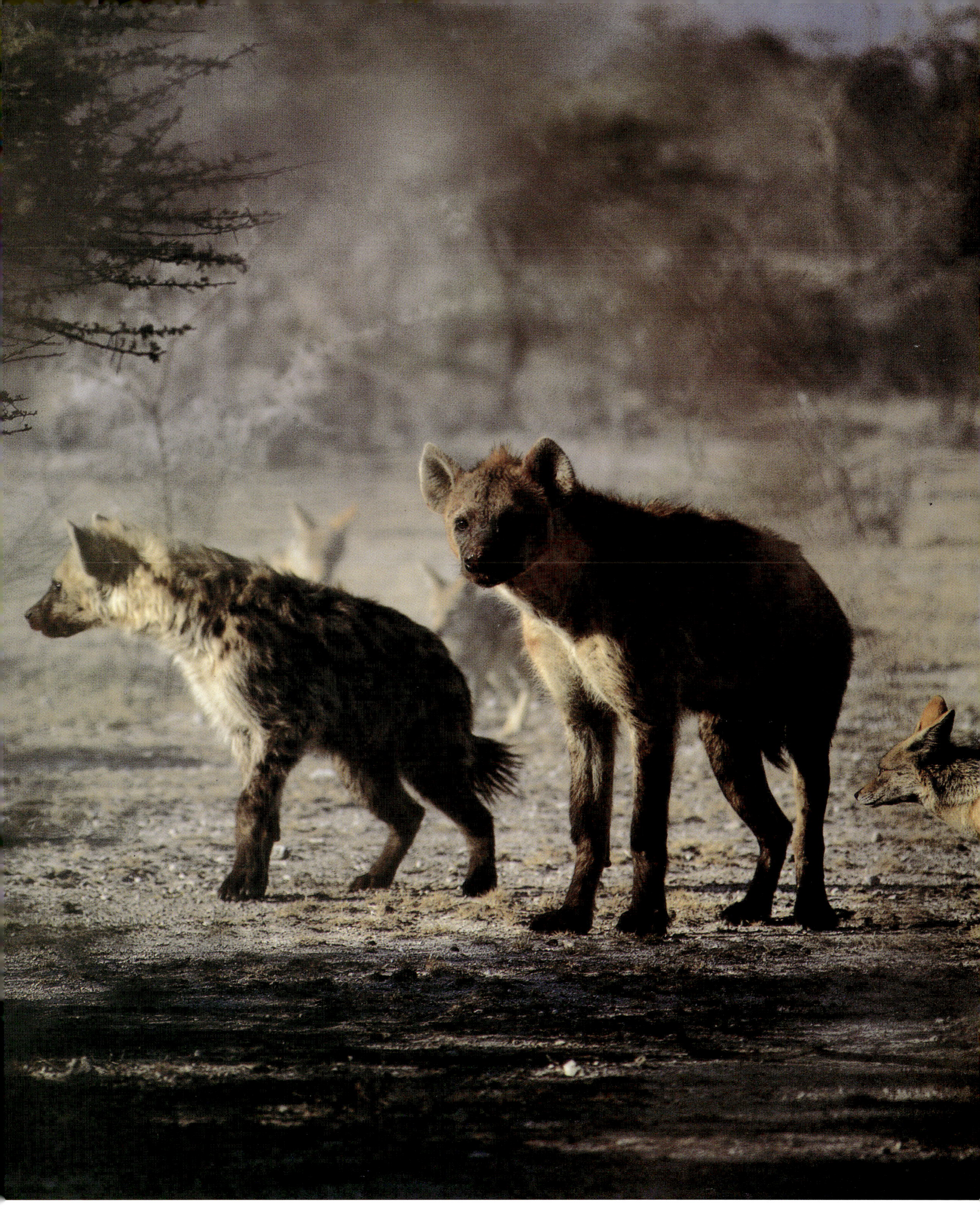

Skulking spotted hyaena gangsters leave few scraps for the scavenging jackals. The hyaena's immensely powerful jaws, more powerful for body size than any other mammal, can crush bones.

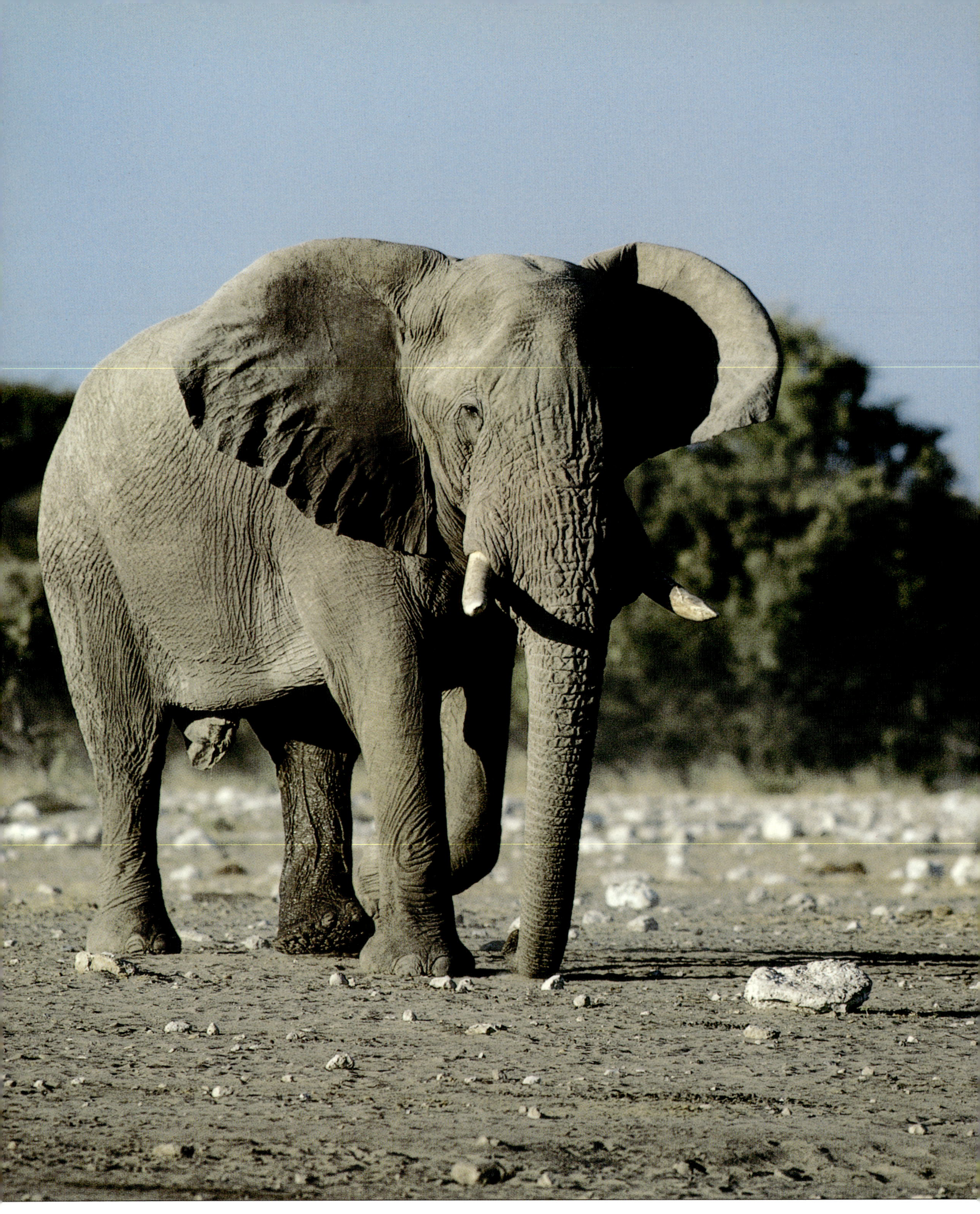

Namibia's elephants, reputedly the tallest in Africa, generally have short, broken tusks, the result of mineral-deficient soil and the need to dig up sand and rocks in their search for roots and water.

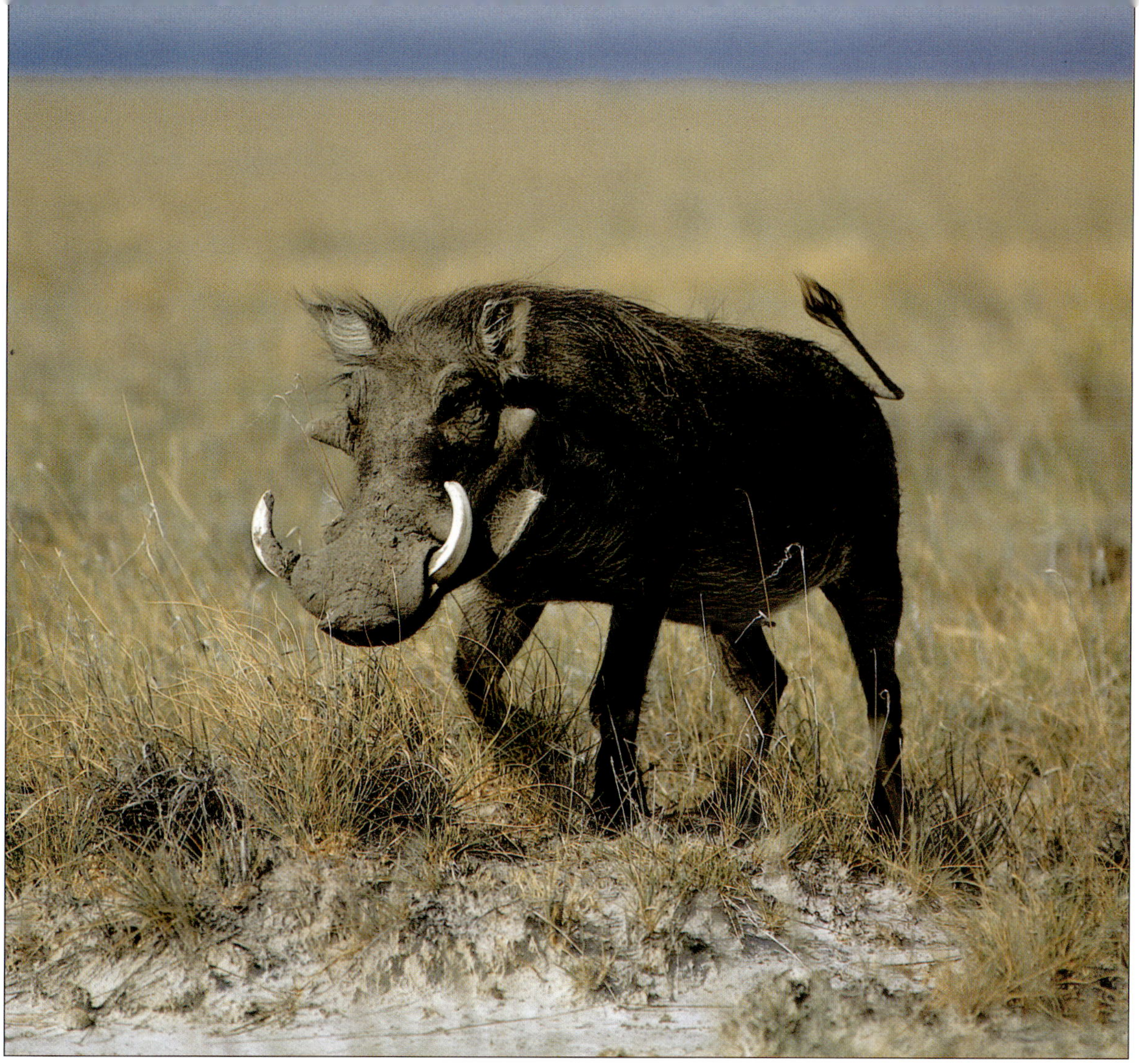

Warthogs are contradictory characters - one minute arrogant kingpin, the next amusing clown. This guy may be off guard now but at the first whiff of danger he will scoot away, tail at full mast.

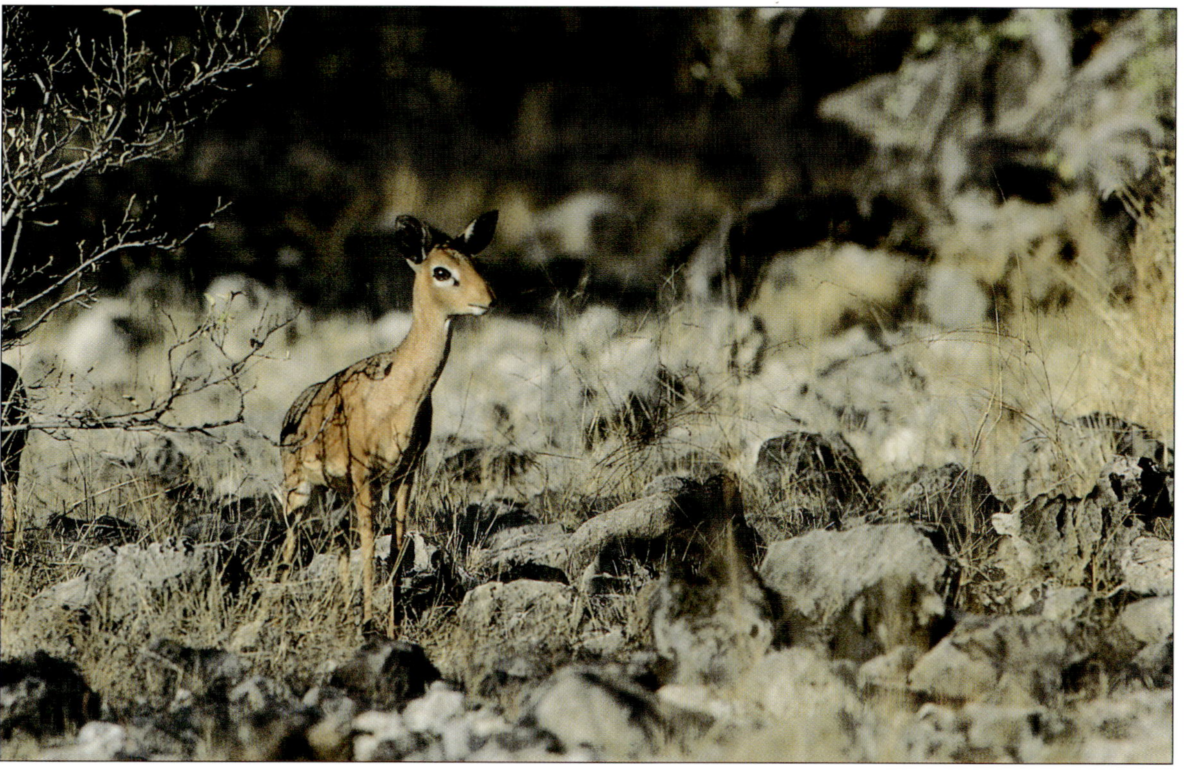

There's no daintier wildlife representative than the Damara dik dik, a Lilliputian-like antelope that stands at no more than 394 millimetres (male) or 386 millimetres (female).

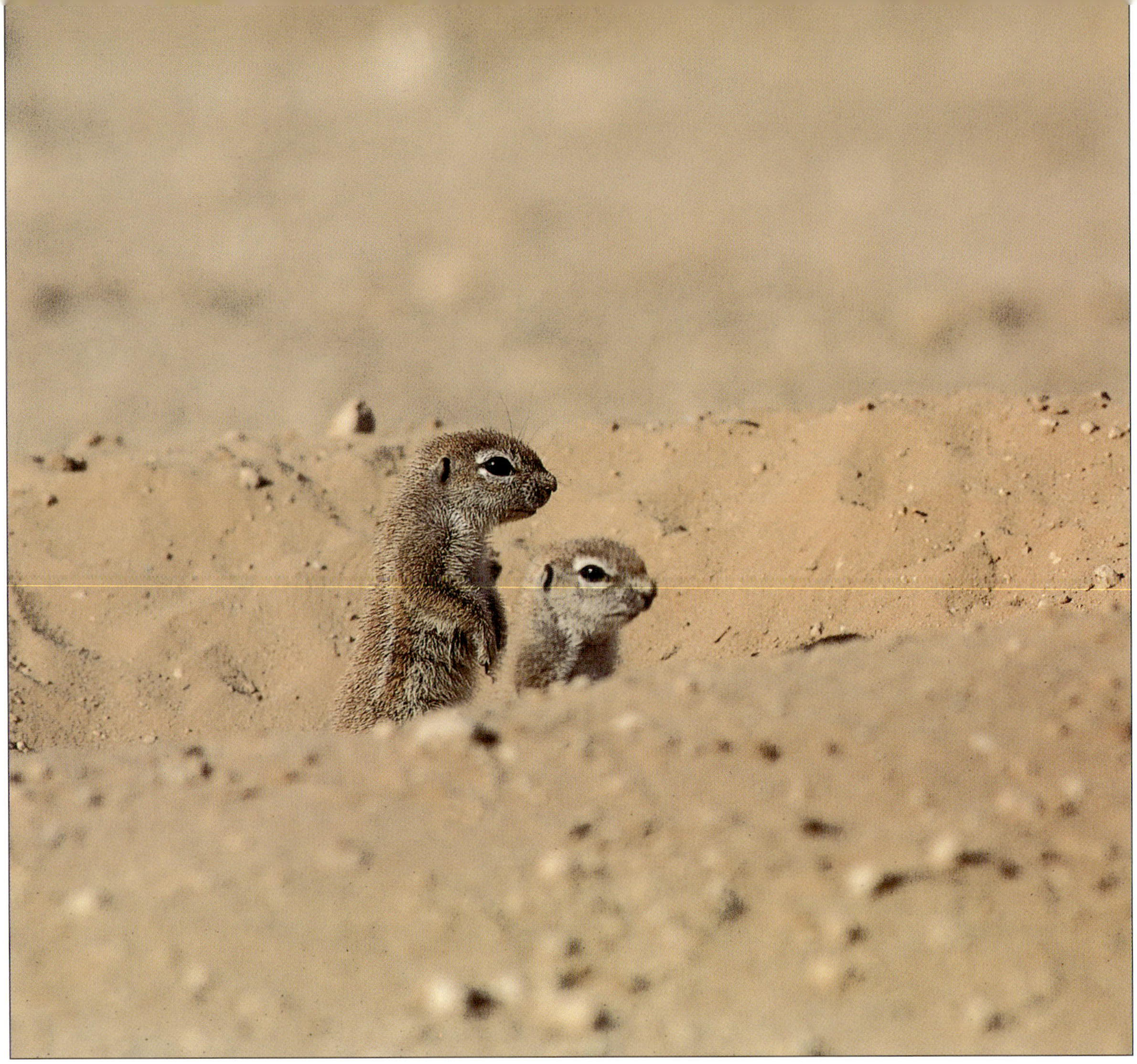

Sociable ground squirrels, like this inquisitive duo at Etosha, often share their underground burrows with yellow mongoose. They are busy inhabitants in arid habitats throughout the country.

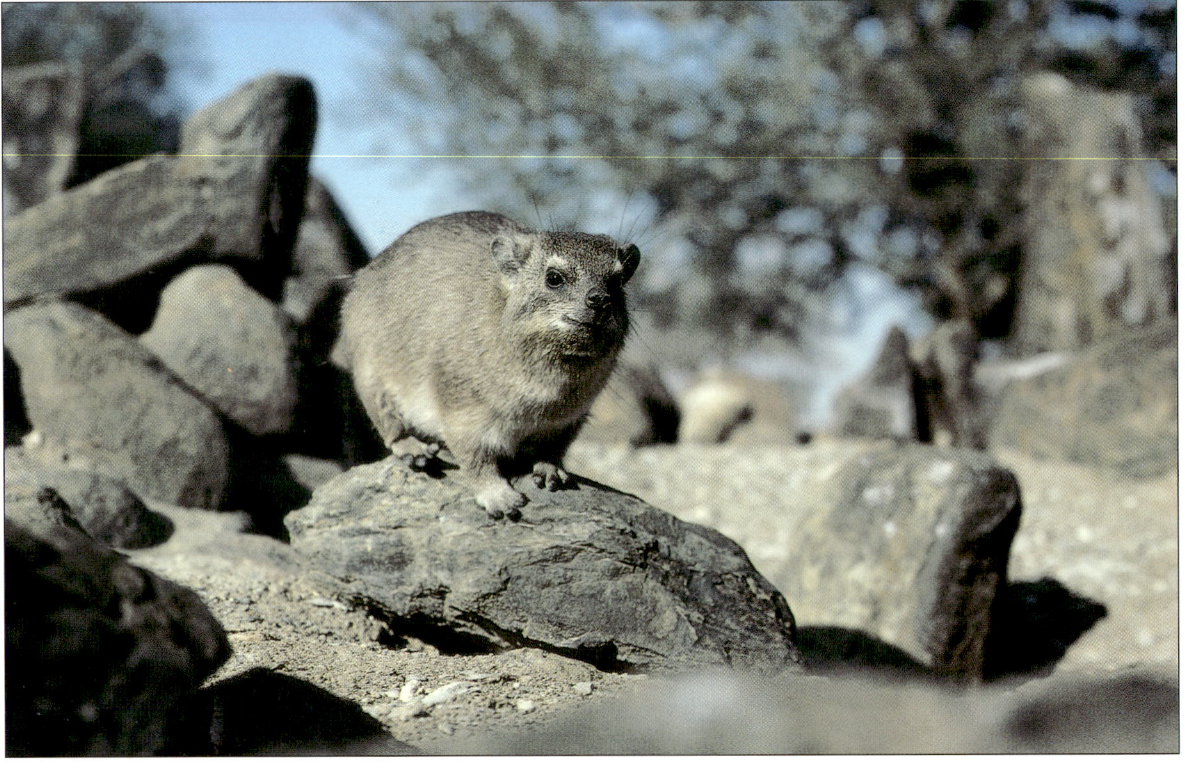

The beady-eyed rock dassie, or hyrax, is the elephant's closest living relative but when it comes to personality the two don't have much in common.

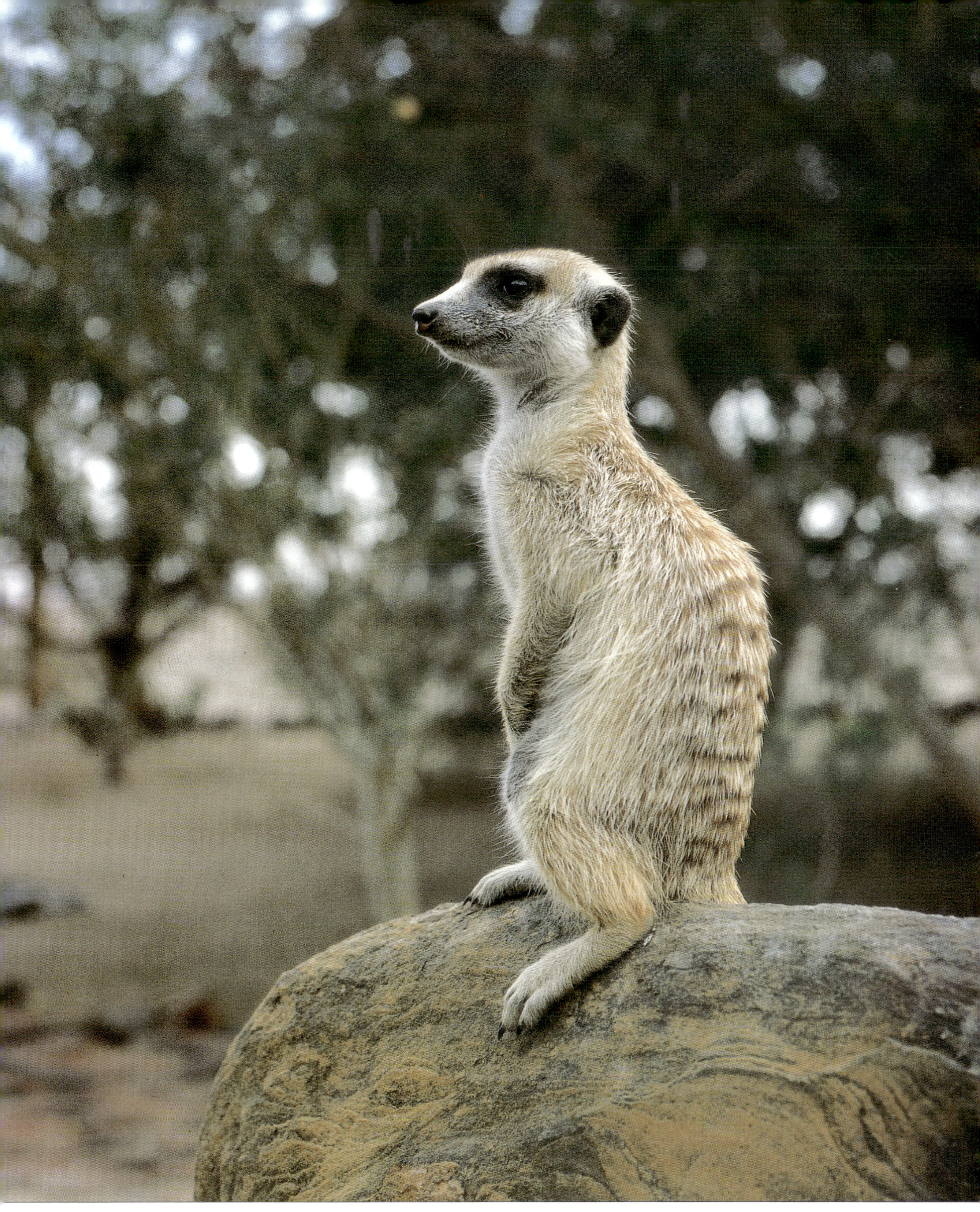

The meerkats are crowd-pleasing performers at the Gariganus farm. In keeping with their wildlife instincts, there is always a guard on duty while the rest of the troupe entertains.

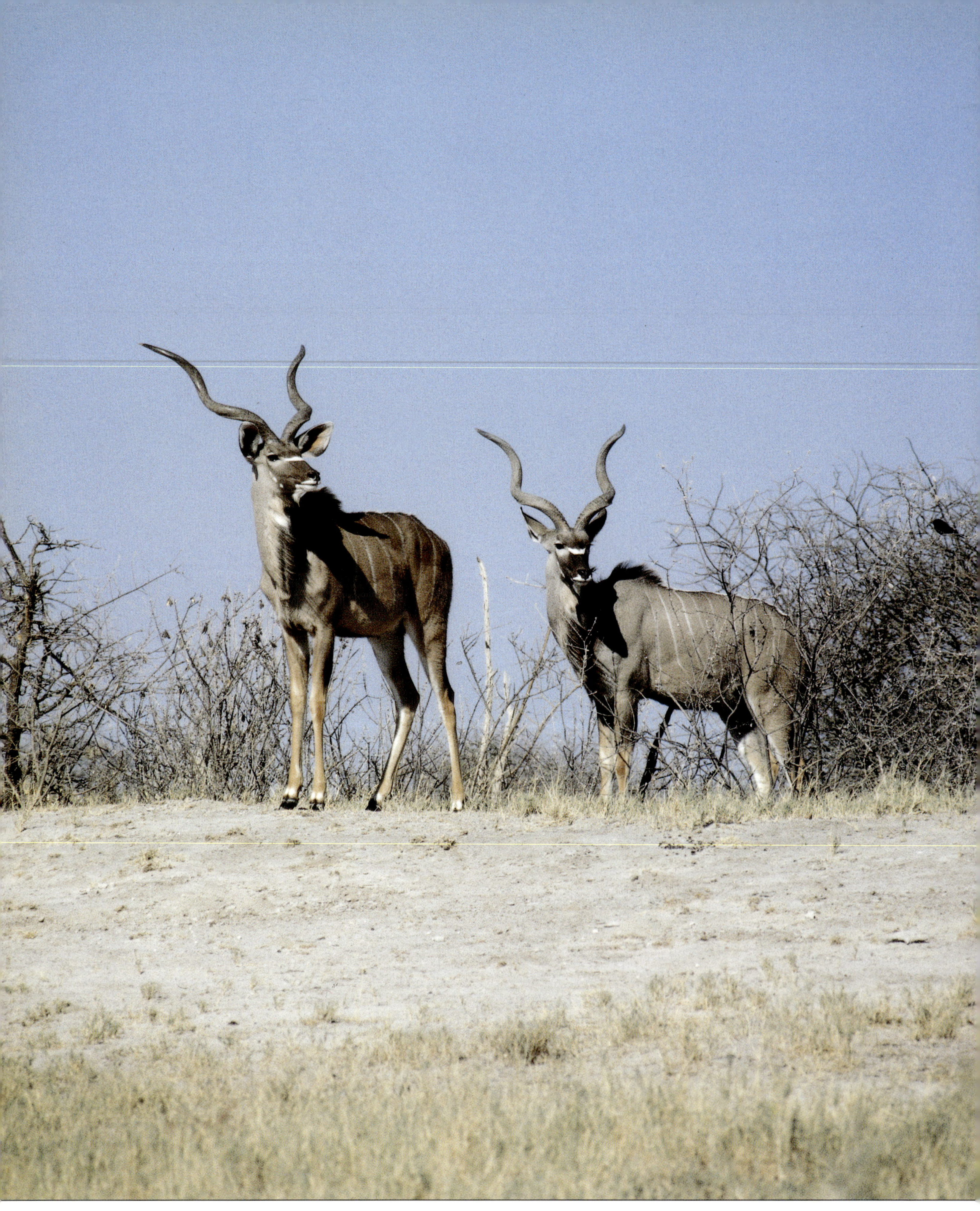

Kudu bulls pause to check the lie of the land as they emerge from the thicket. These regal antelope inhabit the woodlands where their colour makes them difficult to spot.

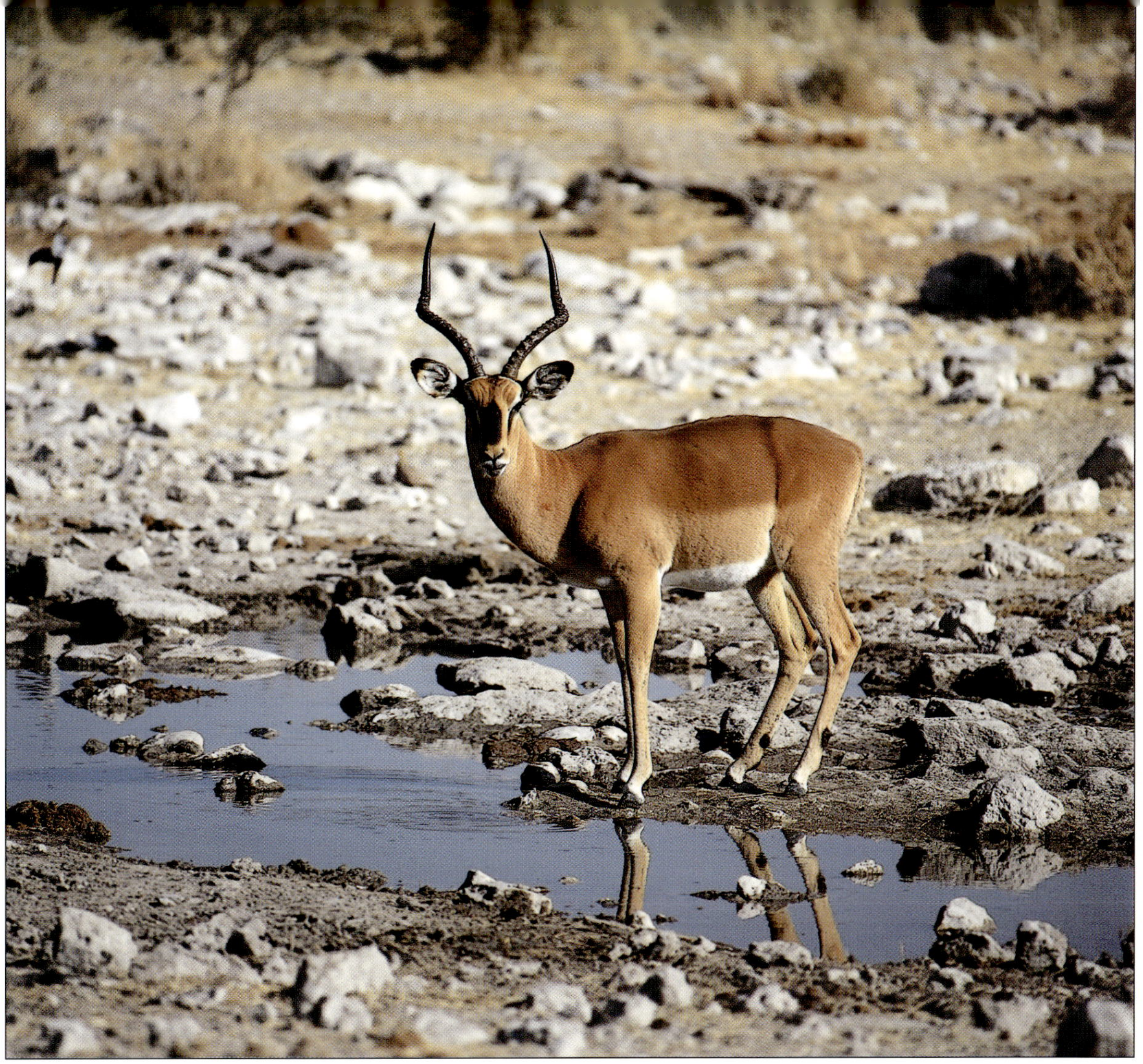

Its dark blaze and reddish-brown colour distinguish the rare black-faced impala, found only in Namibia and south western Angola, from its more widely-scattered impala cousins.

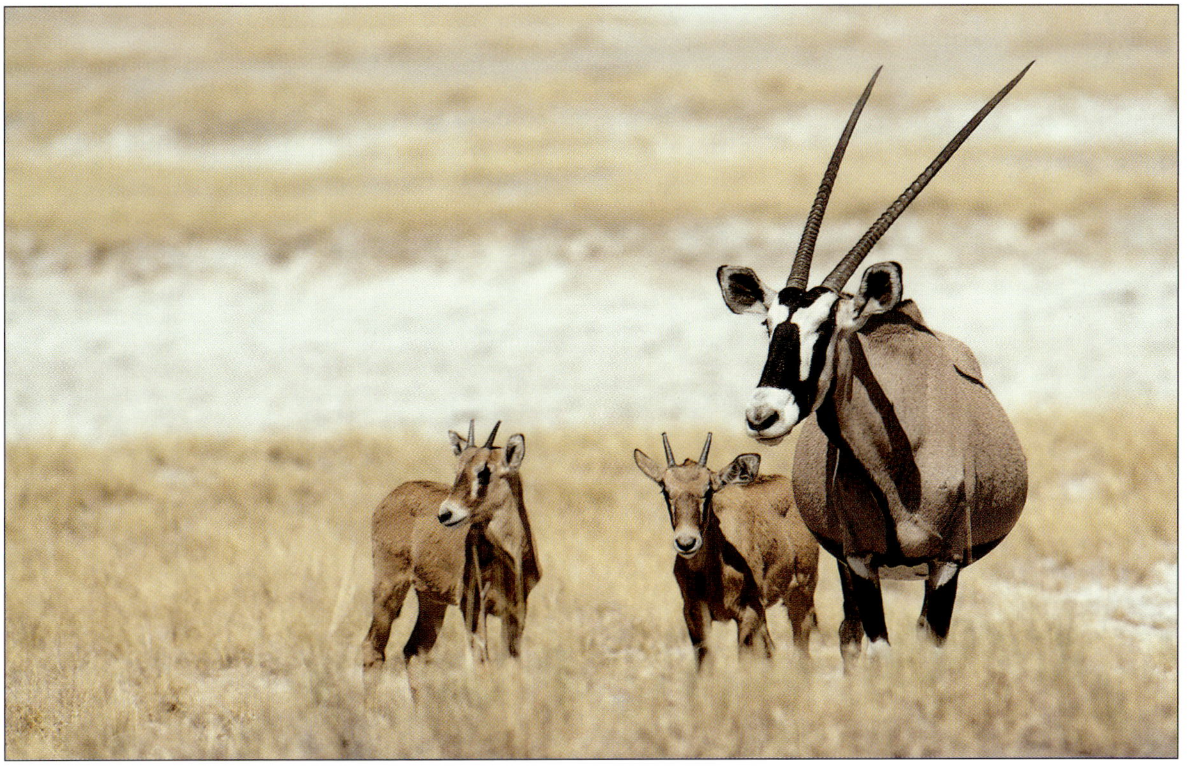

Gemsbok calves stay in hiding for up to six weeks after birth before joining a nursing herd with mother. The distinctive horns of both male and female can grow to 1.2 metres.

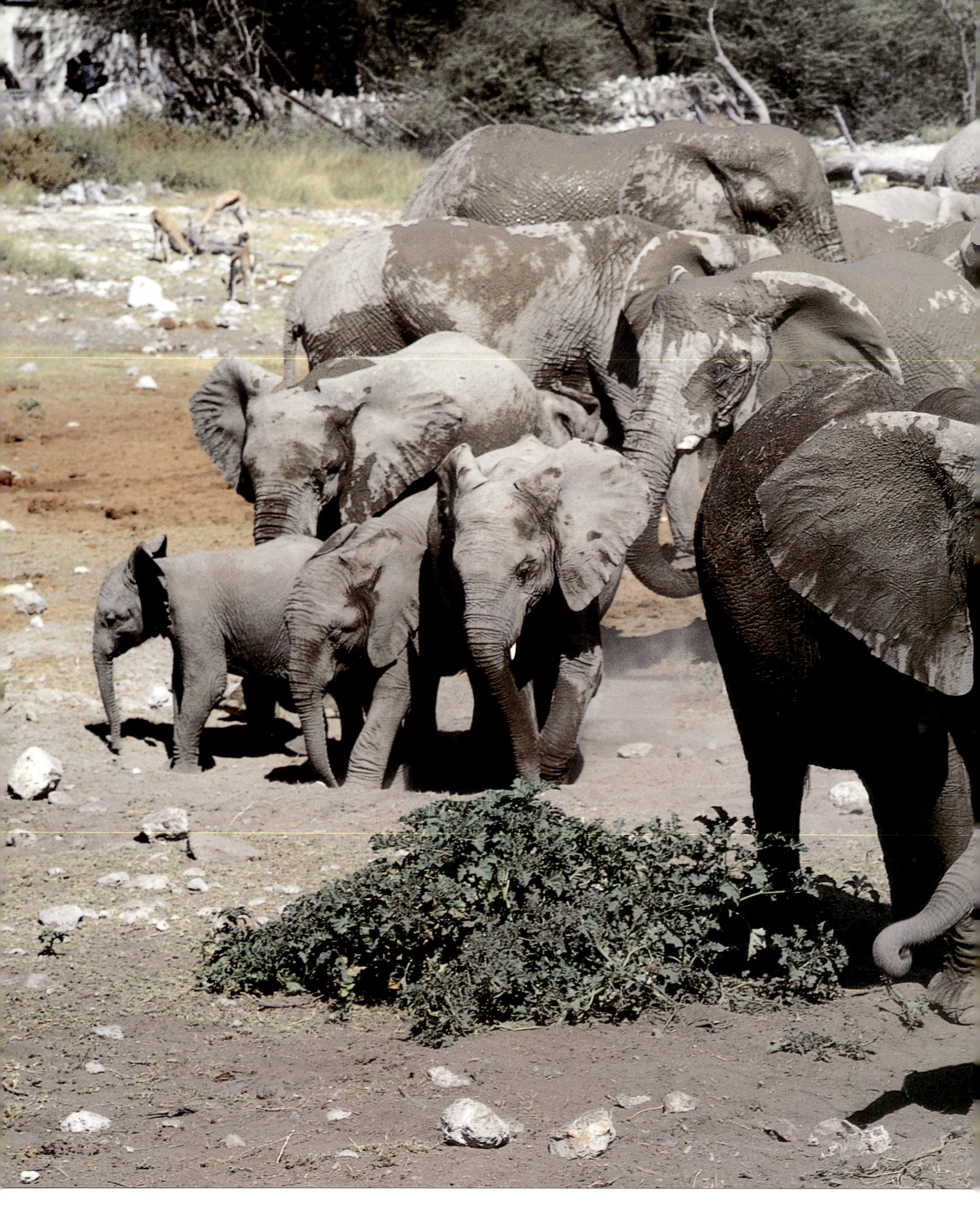

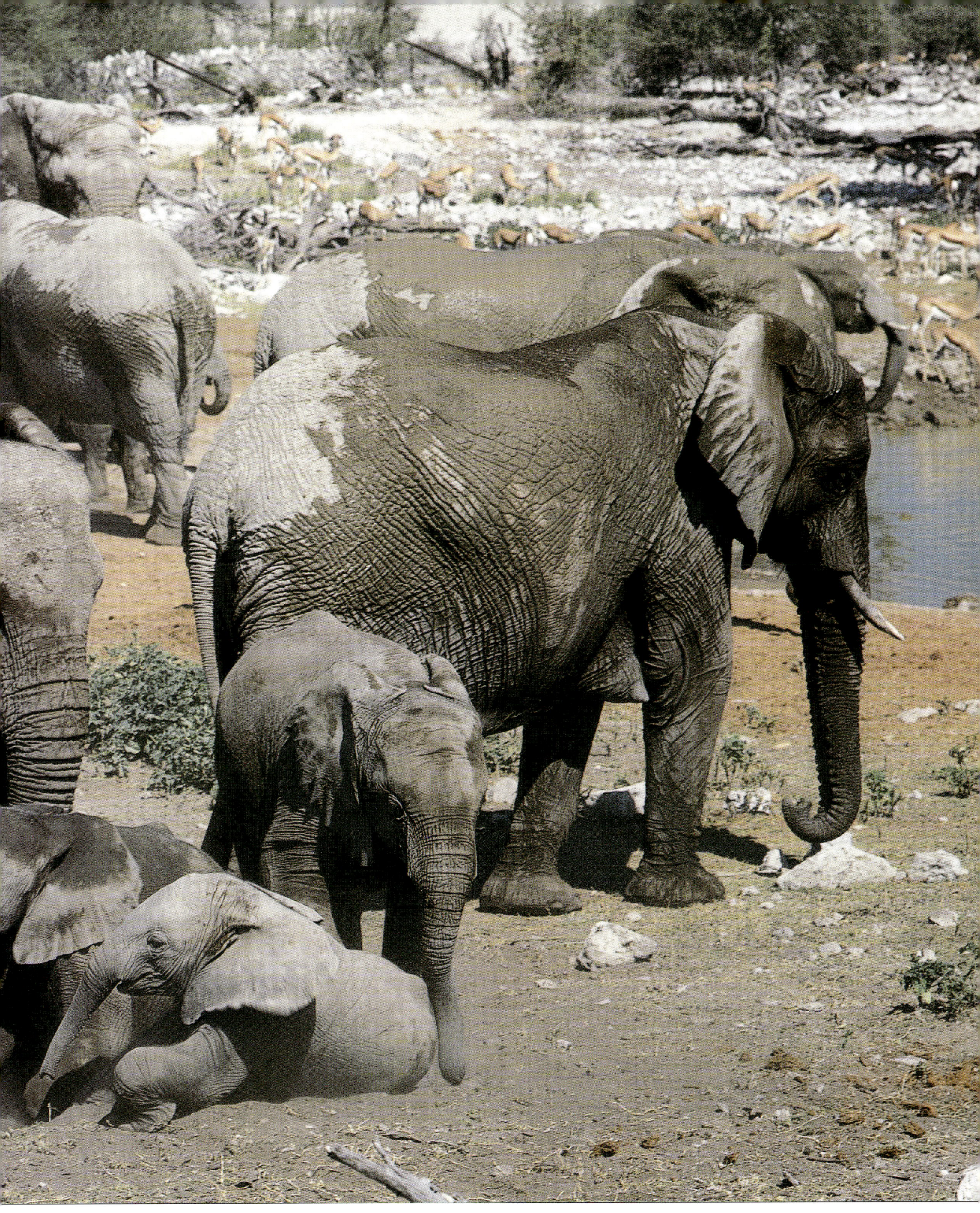

Whether lolling about together at their neighbourhood waterhole in Etosha or looming large and alone from the depths of the Namib desert, Namibia's elephants are a captivating sight.

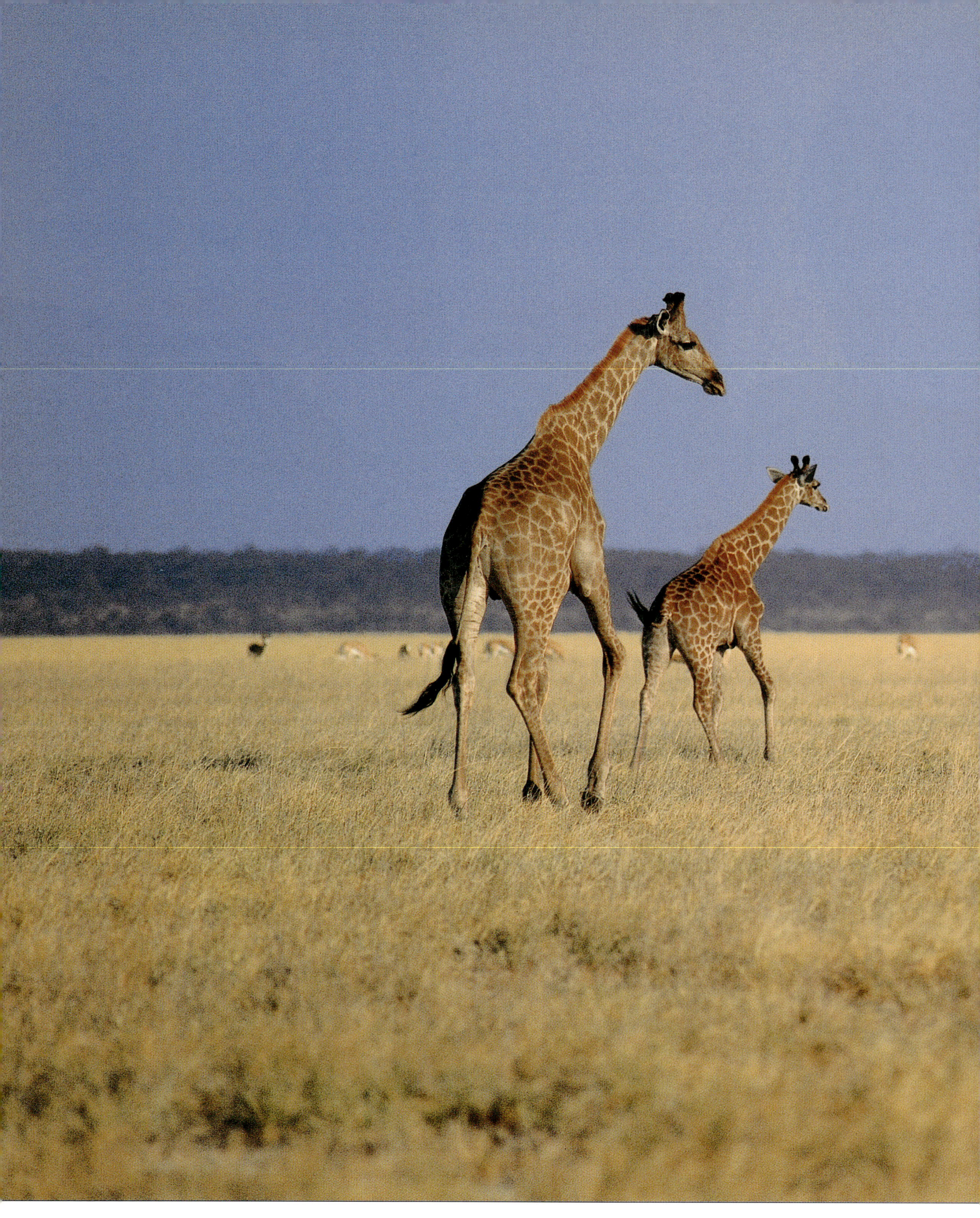

Etosha's Andoni Plains host many grazers, including zebra, wildebeest and gemsbok. It's unusual to see giraffe here but this party has a purpose - they're crossing from one bushveld glade to another.

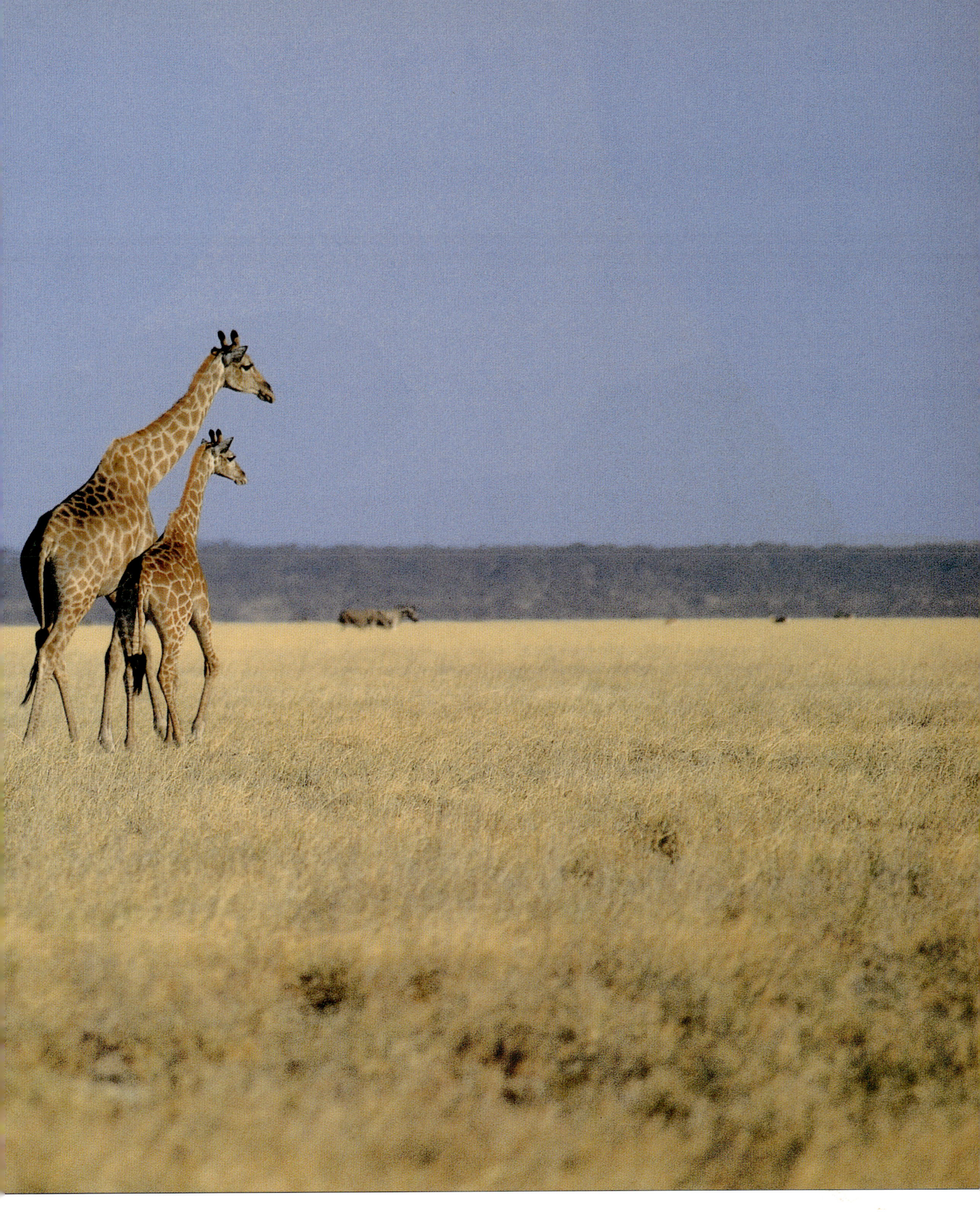

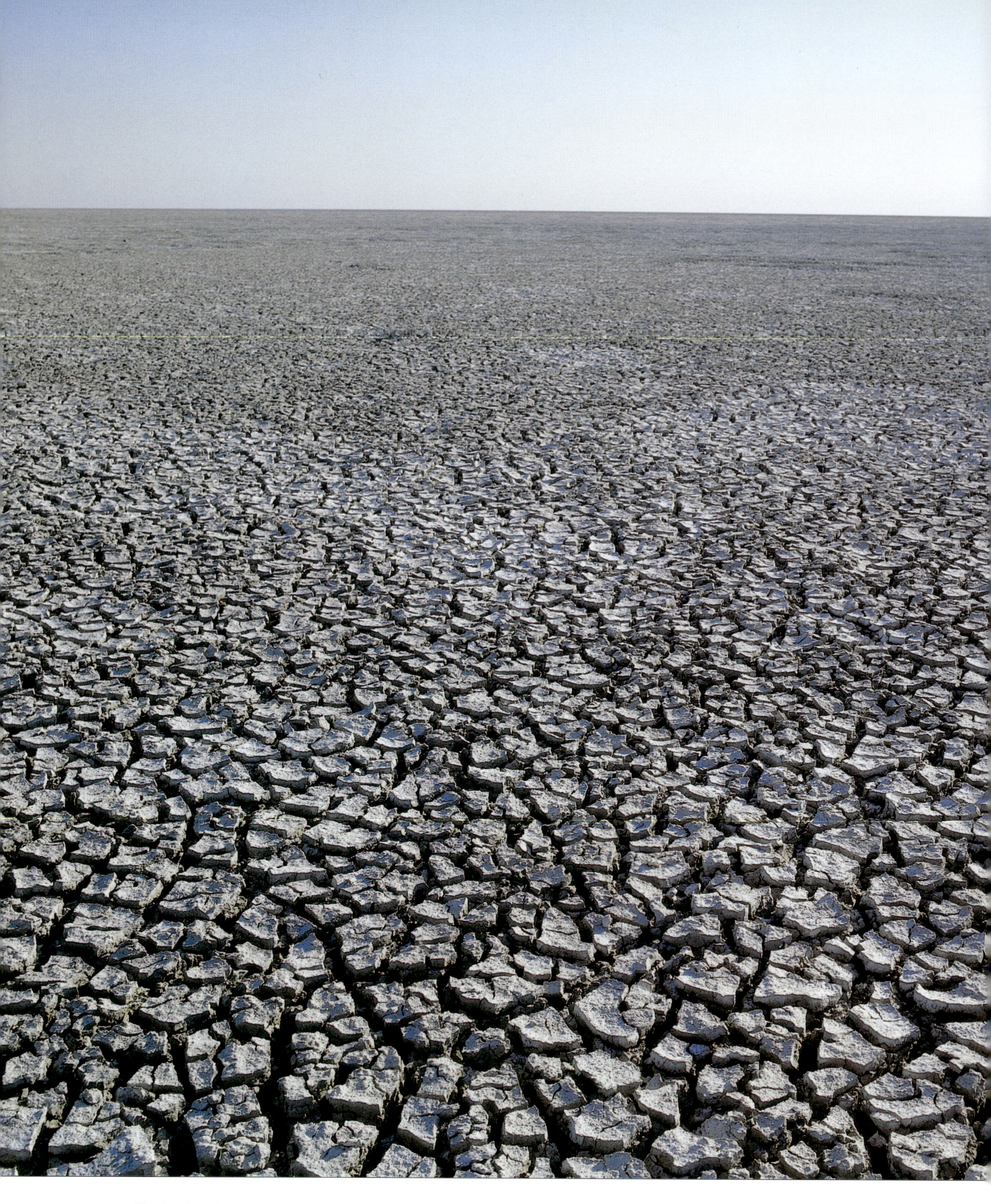

Etosha Pan is the remnant of an ice-age lake. The fractured mosaic of its glimmering sediment shroud is both entrancing and forbidding, inviting and warning those who would dare to cross it.

ETOSHA NATIONAL PARK

Etosha National Park is not just one of the world's last great wildernesses; it is also one of the great bolt-holes for escaping the world. Home to vast herds of zebra, antelope and wildebeest, hunting haunt of lion, leopard and cheetah, stamping ground for large numbers of elephant and giraffe and sanctuary to one of the world's most endangered mammals, the black rhino, Etosha enriches the senses and soothes the soul. Sights - baby elephants frolicking at the waterhole, sounds - lions roaring in the dead of night, and scents – musky air wafting from the open savannah, engulf visitors, transporting them to another realm where nature and its beasts reign supreme. The variety and volume of wildlife roaming this 22,000 square kilometre kingdom make for some of the easiest game viewing in Africa. The floodlit waterholes at Okaukuejo and Halali restcamps, along with Namutoni's historic fort, offer magical viewing experiences at the end of magical days.

The park takes its name from Etosha Pan - a 'Great White Place of Dry Water'. The 6,000 square kilometre calcrete depression occupying the heart of the park was once a large, shallow inland lake but remorseless climatic changes caused it to evaporate rapidly, leaving in its wake brittle, barren, salt-encrusted clay. Nowadays, the Pan, 120 kilometres at its longest and 72 kilometres at its widest, is only rarely awash with water. When that happens, flocks of flamingos, as many as a million birds, descend en masse reminiscent of an earlier era when the Pan sustained abundant life.

Etosha is also habitat to the hardy moringa tree which usually grows on rocky slopes such as those around Halali. Hundreds of specimens are grouped in a forest on a sandy plain west of Okaukuejo.

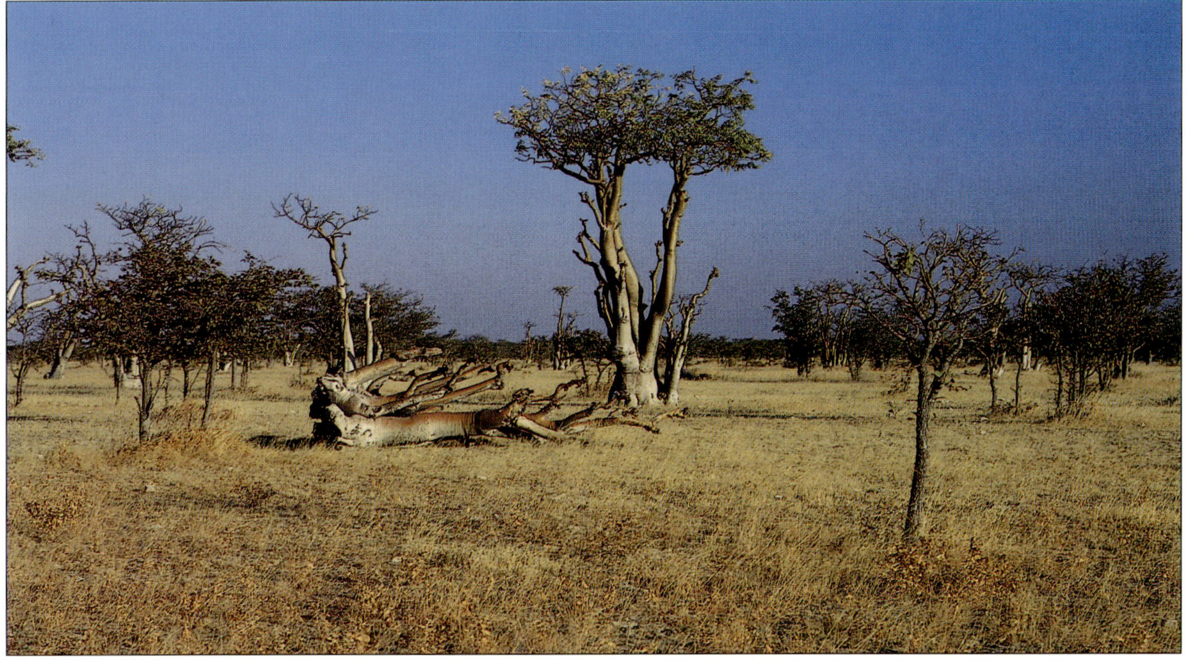

According to San legend, God tossed these misshapen moringa trees head-first into the ground after He finished creating the Universe, thus giving rise to the Sprokieswoud, or Haunted Forest.

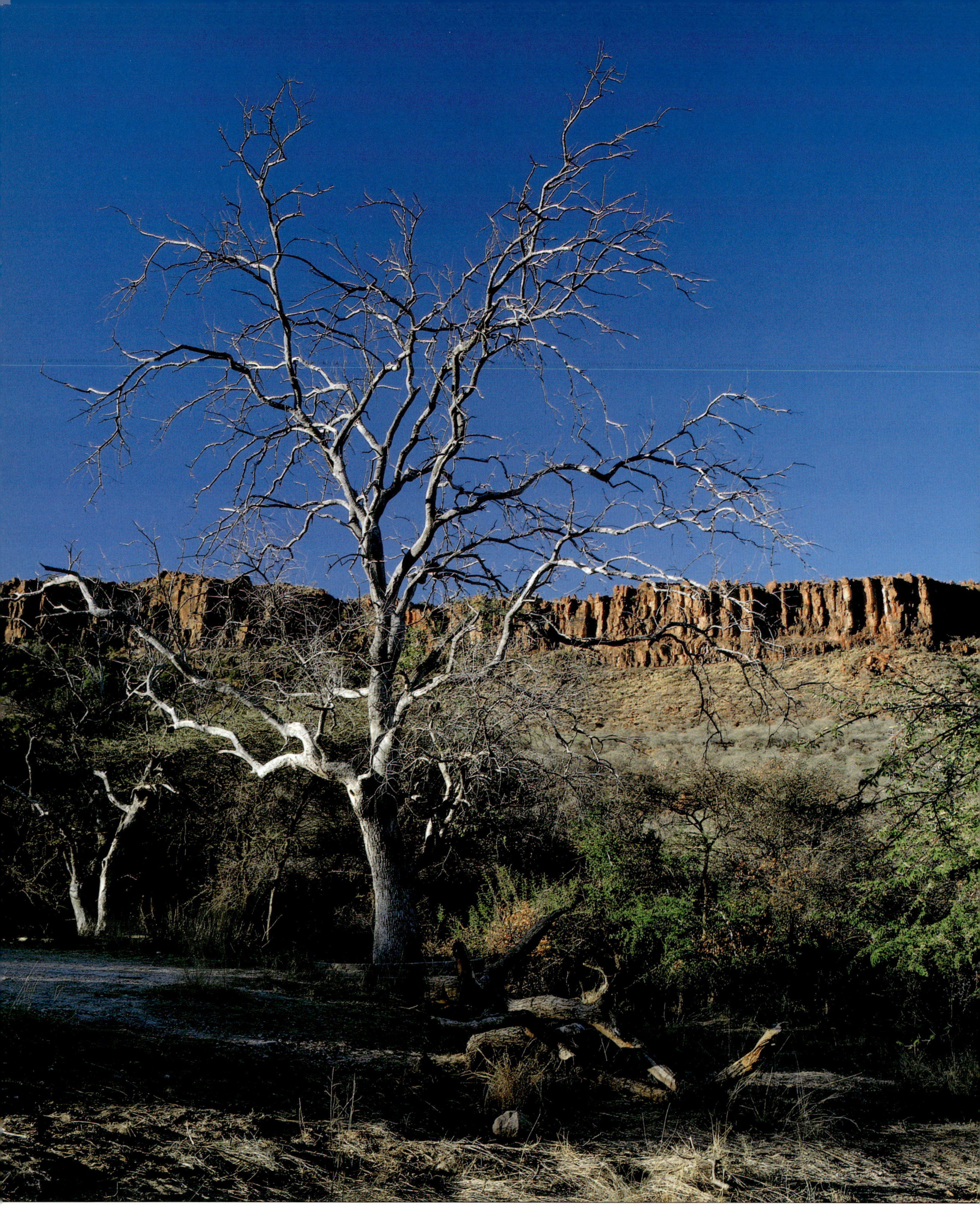

Stunning red mountain faces, composed of Etjo sandstone, provide a startling backdrop to the pleasant Bernabé de la Bat restcamp at Waterberg Plateau Park.

WATERBERG PLATEAU

The deeply fissured cliff-face of the Okarukavisa Mountains rises like a fortress above the Waterberg Plateau where millions of years ago dinosaurs roamed dense woodlands and bountiful plains. However, the geological history of this spectacular escarpment predates even the Mesozoic wildlife. Millions of years earlier Namibia was part of the super-continent known as Gondwana, a gigantic land mass, including Antarctica, huddled near the South Pole. In other words, Namibia lay within the earth's ice zone and was almost completely covered by inland glaciers. When the African section of Gondwanaland cut loose from the South Pole and drifted north about 280 million years ago these glaciers melted, beginning a phenomenal climatic change. Within 100 million years the ice masses had metamorphosed from, first, glacial lakes to, eventually, seas of sand dunes. The dune sands subsequently petrified into sandstone, known as the Etjo sandstone, which nowadays can be seen in Namibia's vivid red rock outcrops as illustrated so dramatically at Waterberg.

Later, tectonic upheaval in the area caused the ancient Damara Mountains to thrust upward spilling their age-hardened rocks over the layers of sediment that had been deposited during the area's transition from icecap to sand dune. Thus, shielded from savage erosion, Waterberg survived as the high plateau of today. The 200-metre high Okarukavisa Mountains are the result of pronounced upward tilting in that corner of the plateau.

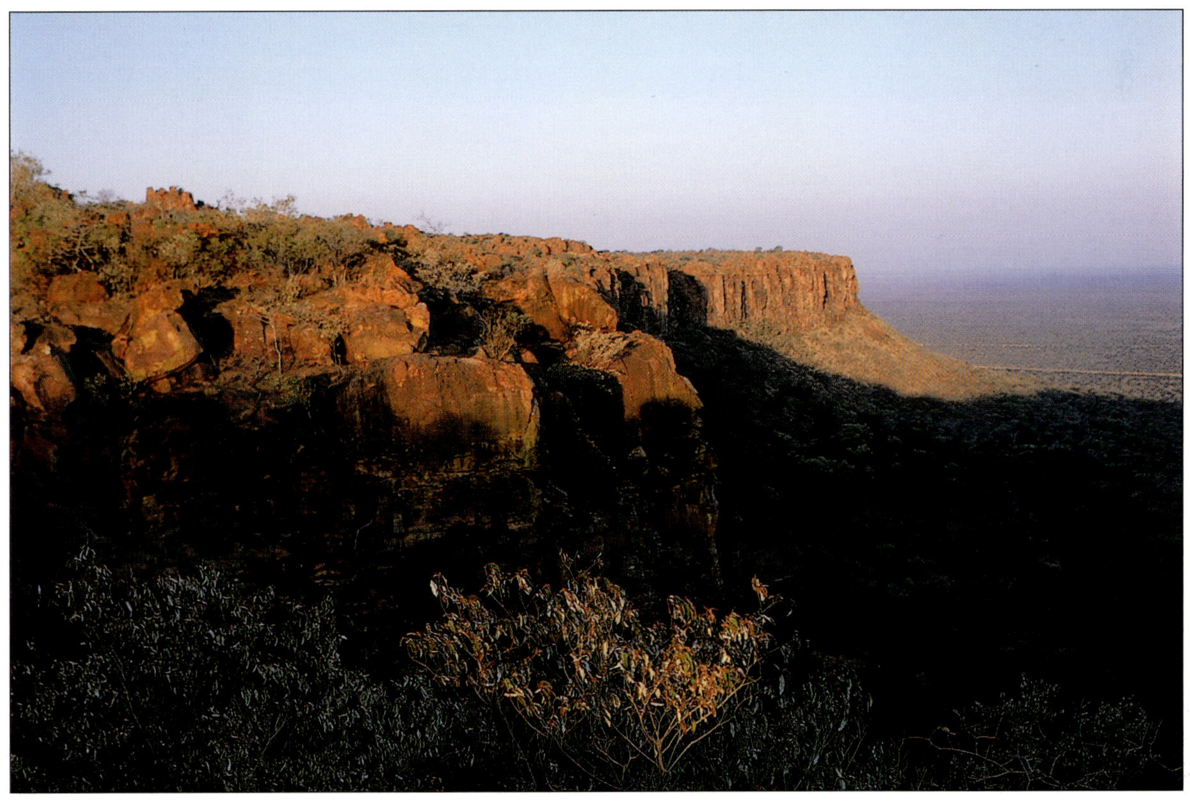

Basking in the warm glow of late afternoon sunlight, the Okarukavisa Mountains rise above levelled plains that stretch all the way from the Waterberg Plateau to the Kalahari Desert.

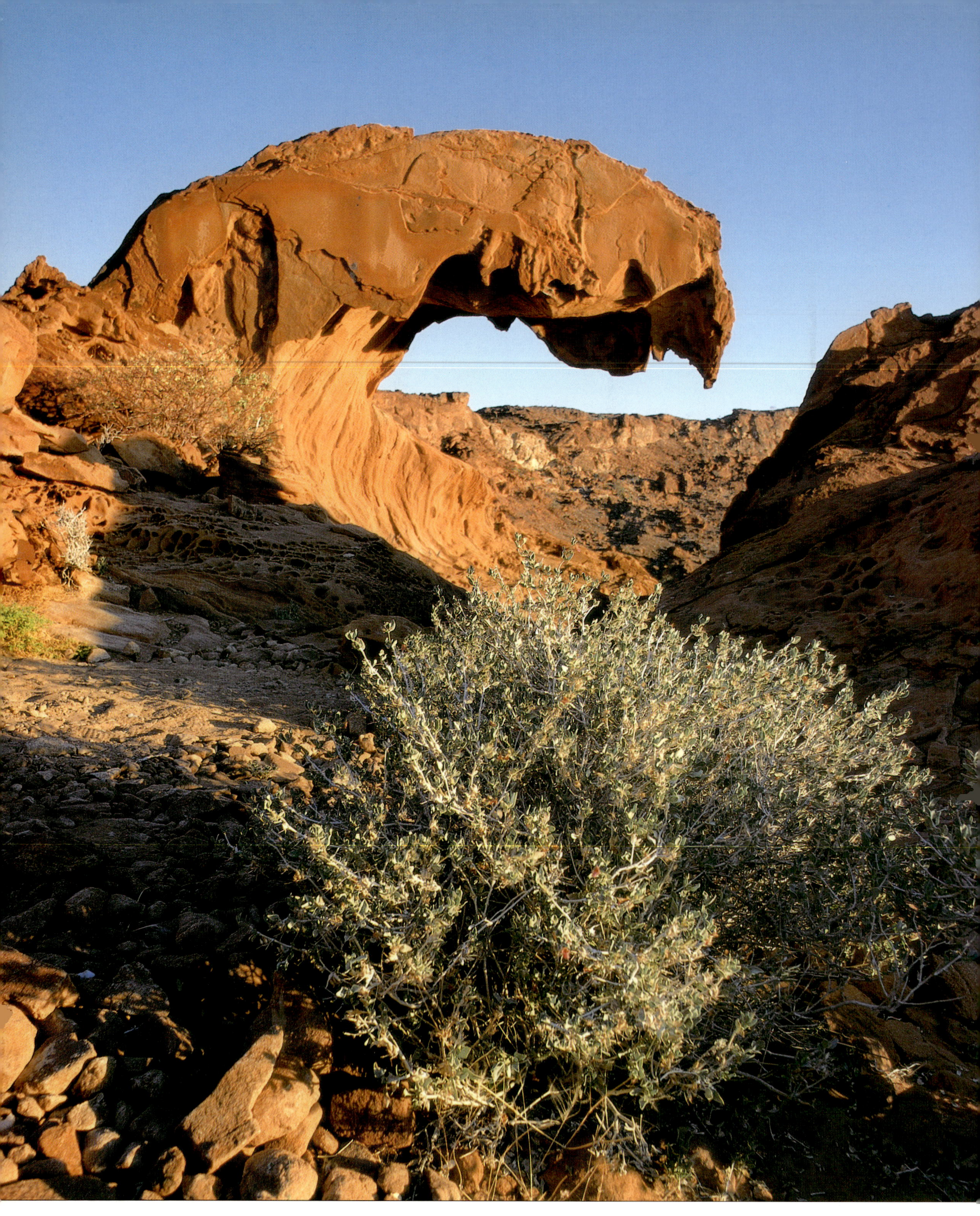

The forces of nature over several millennia have fashioned Namibia's landscape, twisting and turning the terrain, carving out spectacular shapes such as the 'Lion's Jaw' found at Twyfelfontein.

TWYFELFONTEIN - OUTDOOR MUSEUM

Water has always been an unreliable resource at Twyfelfontein, a valley where impressive red rock formations lie in chaos across sandstone terraces. During good rains the groundwater dams up in the porous sandstone layer, unable to permeate the harder seam of shale underneath, and creates a spring. But in these arid conditions good rains are few and far between, hence the name Twyfelfontein meaning 'Doubtful Spring'. There is little doubt, however, that the extensive collection of ancient rock engravings on display in Twyfelfontein's open-air museum is one of the finest in Africa. Around 2,400 astonishingly accurate petroglyphs are believed to have been painstakingly chiselled into the smooth rock surfaces nearly 6,000 years ago by ancestors of the San bushmen.

Continuous erosion over millions of years crafted the choice rock surfaces on which the artists etched their remarkable illustrations. First, deep rivers gouged through ancient desert deposits to create wide canyons bordered by table mountain ranges. These ranges then shed huge sandstone boulders into valleys such as Twyfelfontein. The crashing rocks split asunder at natural fissures exposing flat, soft, fine-grain surfaces composed from petrified desert sands - ready and waiting to be engraved by the Stone Age artists.

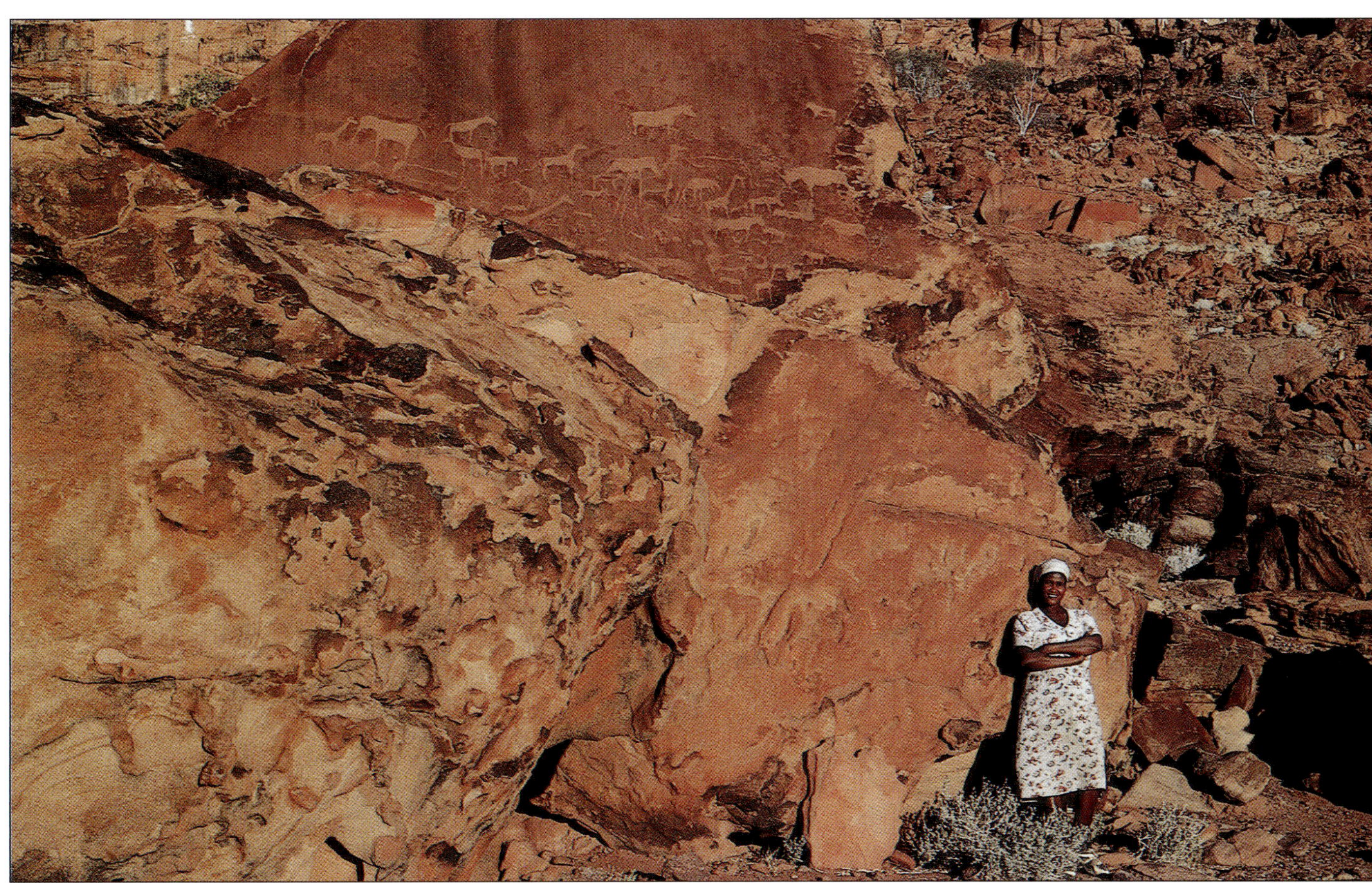

Guide Elsie illuminates the rich red boulders that gave the Bushmen artists their canvases around 6,000 years ago. Many engravings are clearly visible on the face of the top boulder.

THE STONE AGE SAN MAN

During the Stone Age, San bushmen roamed Namibia. Their hunter-gatherer culture prevailed until as recently as the early 1900s when small groups of San remained scattered throughout the country. Although they had distinctly different cultures and languages these groups shared the same hunting lifestyle and rapport with nature. But within less than a century, the San's total adherence to their traditional hunter-gatherer way of life had disappeared, overtaken by persecution, assimilation into other cultural groups and the loss of traditional hunting grounds.

The illustrations on display in Twyfelfontein's Stone Age art gallery give a glimpse not only of the life of the early San hunter-gathers, but also of the impact the changing climate had on birds and animals found in the area at that time. The forebears of today's wildlife are well represented with giraffe, rhinoceros, zebra and ostrich all portrayed in large numbers. However, while there are many recordings of gemsbok and springbok, almost a quarter of the engravings depict unknown antelope. And although Twyfelfontein is 200 kilometres from the coast, illustrations of marine life such as penguins, seals and flamingoes, which are no longer found here, suggest the area may have been inundated with water 6,000 years ago.

The juxtaposition of footprints and handprints, predator and prey, accurate and abstract hieroglyphics leaves visiting art critics guessing at what stories the San might have been telling.

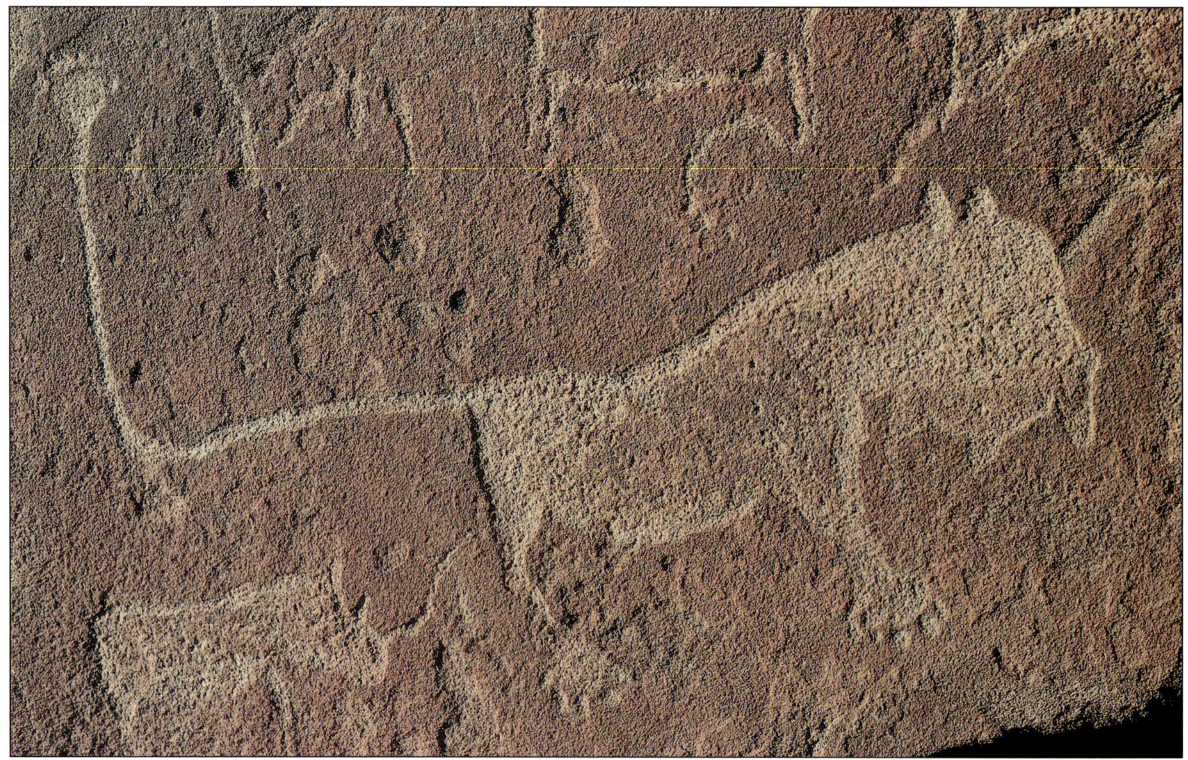

The lion engraving is just one of around 2,400 petroglyphs of beasts encountered by the San some 6,000 years ago. Ancestors of many of the animals depicted still roam the African plains today.

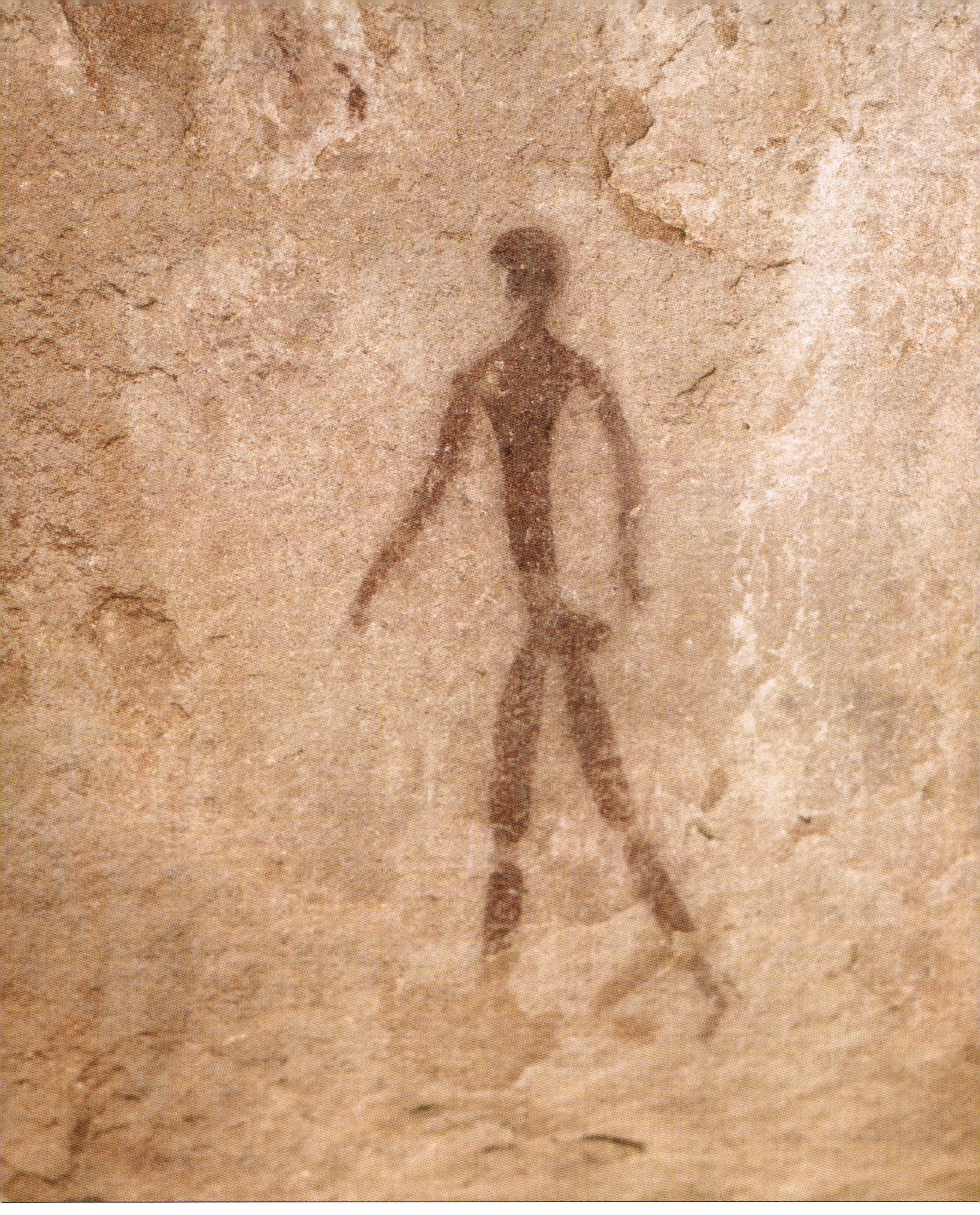

This striking portrait, artist unknown, can be seen on the under-surface within a bushmen's cave-dwelling at Twyfelfontein's open-air art gallery.

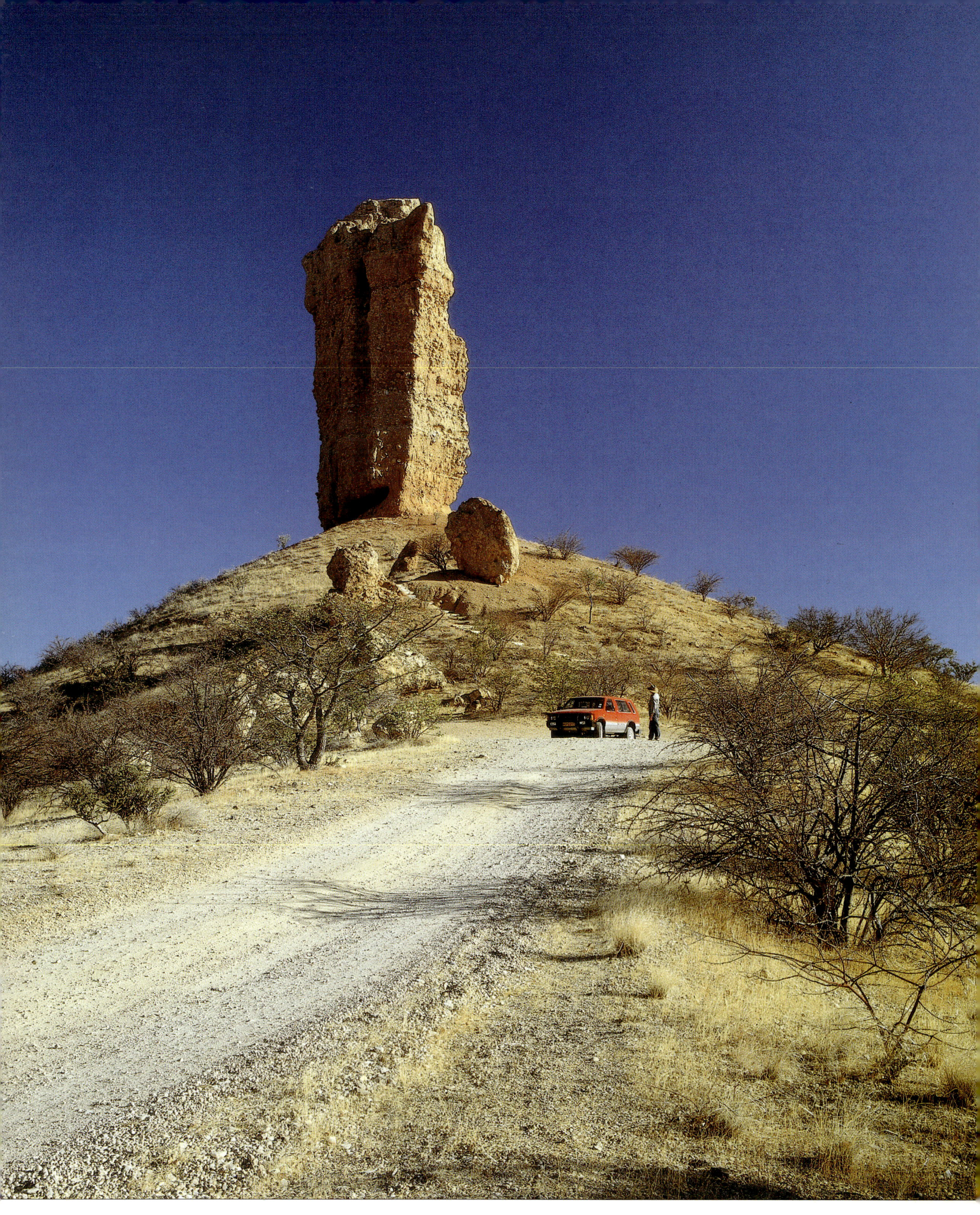

Soaring 35 metres above its pyramid pedestal, the Vingerklip monolith is a lonely relic cut adrift from nearby table-top terraces by savage, relentless erosion over millions of years.

NATURE'S HAND IN EARTH'S HISTORY

To travel the countryside of Namibia is to turn the pages of Earth's history. Fascinating geological features, graphic prototypes from our planet's evolution, provide colour and character at every turn in the road, as in the heat-ravaged, rugged and forsaken Ugab Valley near Khorixas. Here Vingerklip, or the Rock Finger, rises in stern salute above the withered floodplains carved out by the once mighty Ugab River as it coursed to the Atlantic. Vingerklip represents a relatively recent epoch in Namibia's history. Just two million years ago northern ice ages caused the sea level to drop, which prompted the Ugab to flow more aggressively seaward, gouging out its own soft bed laid down over millions of years. Consequently, the river became deeper but narrower and sections of its old course were left high and dry as river terraces. Subsequent erosion by the elements has stranded Vingerklip as a forlorn vestige of the main terrace.

Another of Nature's mysteries, the Petrified Forest is as intriguing as it is incongruous. Its fossilized tree trunks, evidence of extensive woodlands that once covered Namibia, did not, in fact, grow in the inhospitable, sparsely vegetated terrain where they lie. They were uprooted from more fertile soil great distances away and swept to their rocky graves on floods that raged through the countryside around 200 million years ago.

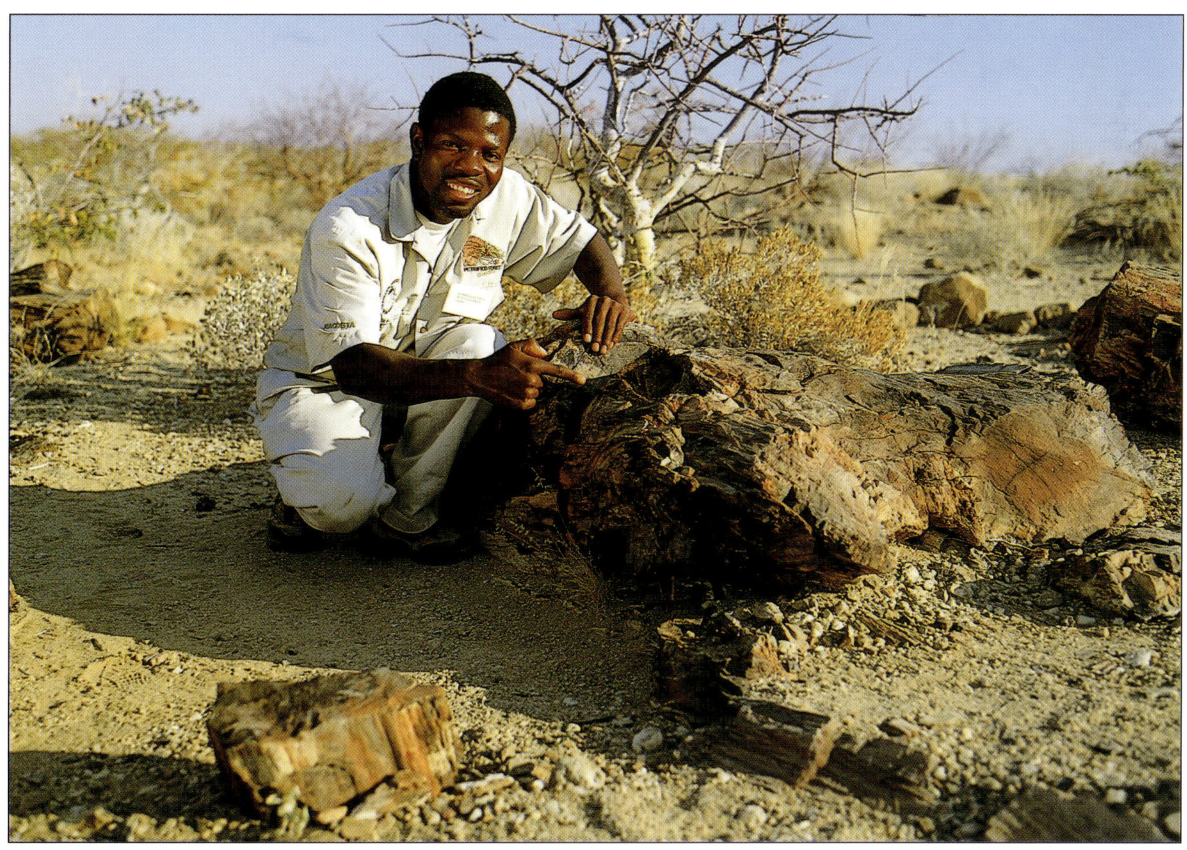

Guide Gabriel points to the carbon logs of the Petrified Forest, which lie like lost pieces of a puzzle, on a desolate, flinty hillside west of Khorixas, far from the rich soil in which they once flourished.

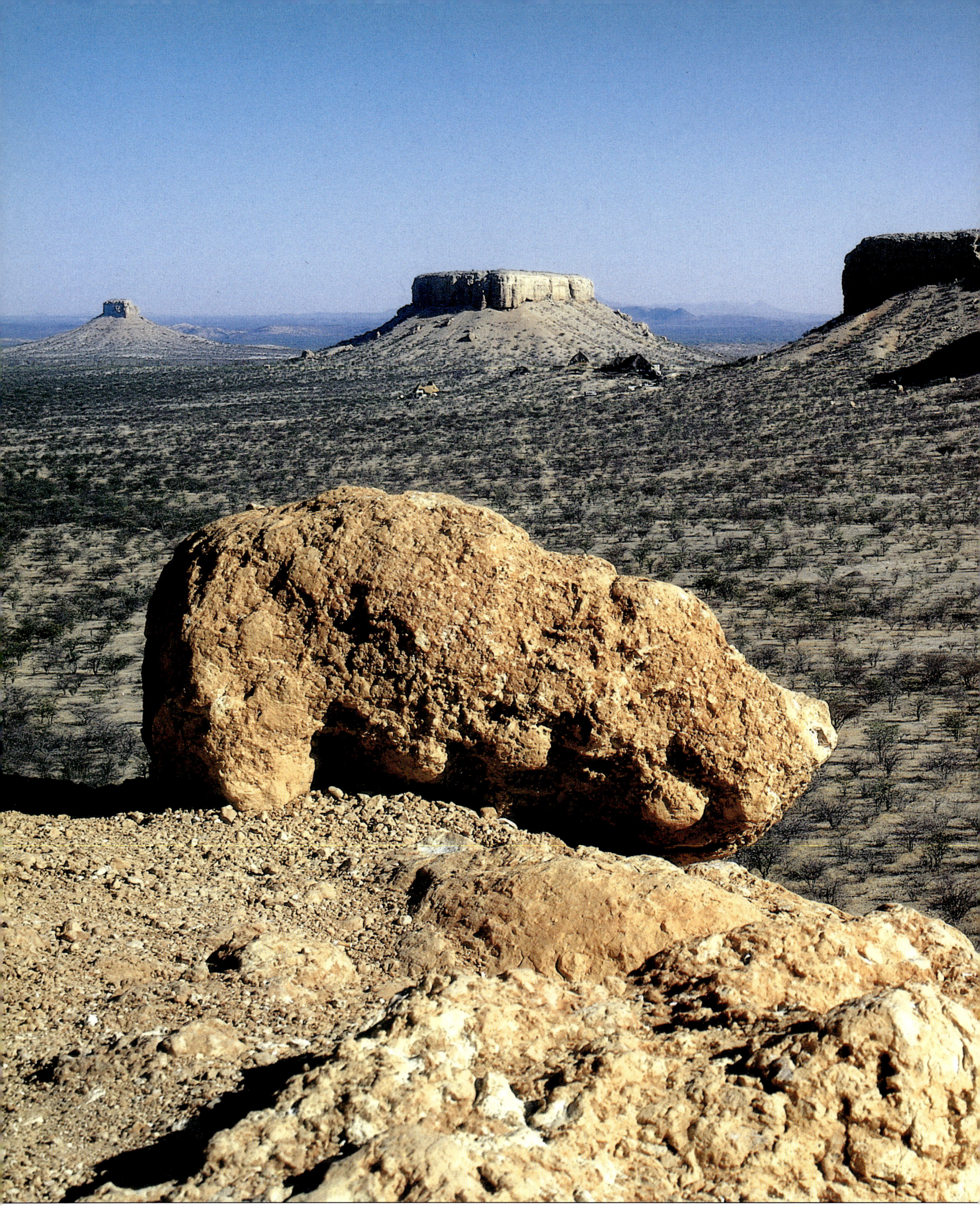

Namibia's countryside is a dramatic chronicle of nature's hand in Earth's history. The Ugab Valley terraces stand sentinel-like above the eroded, waterless riverbed.

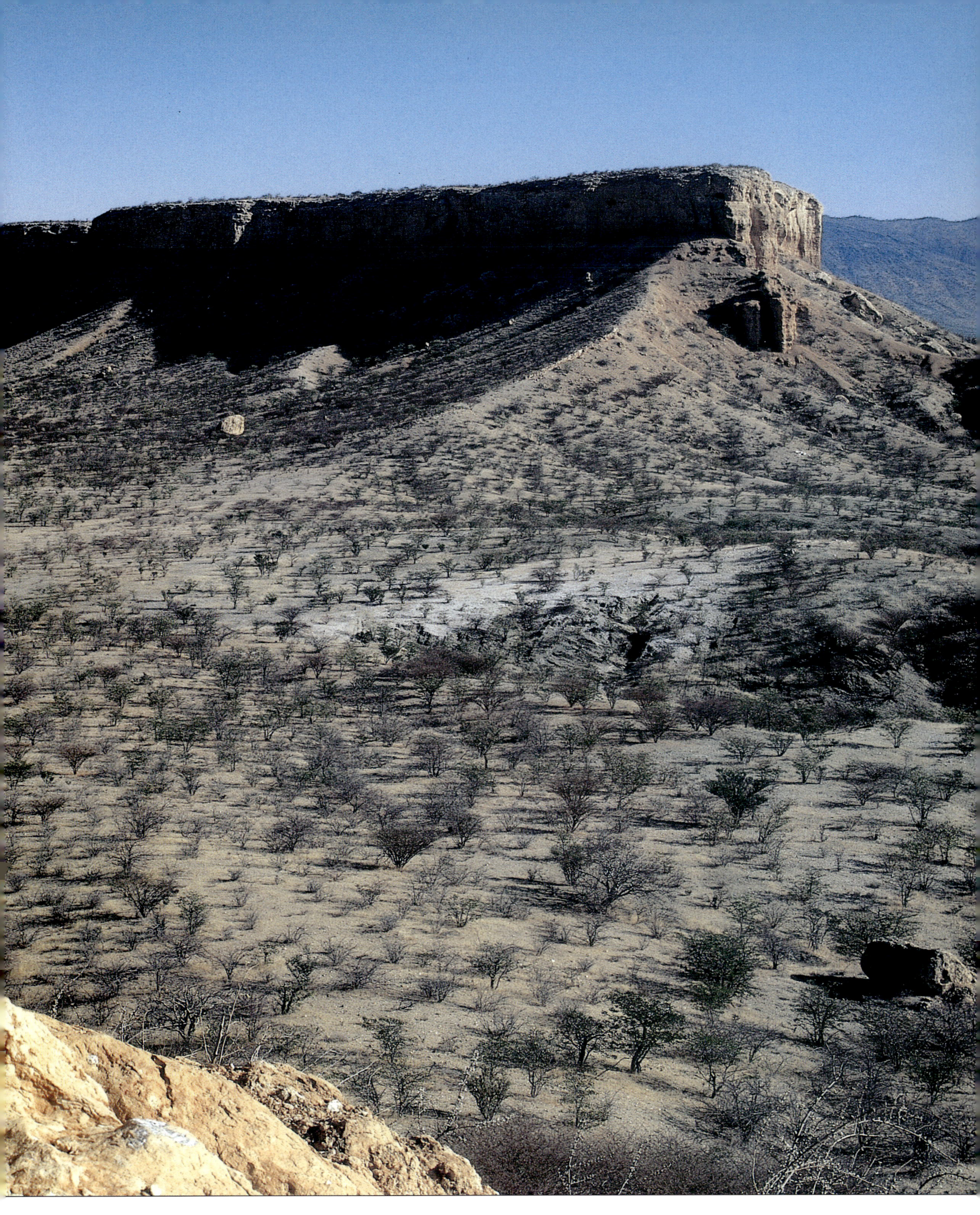

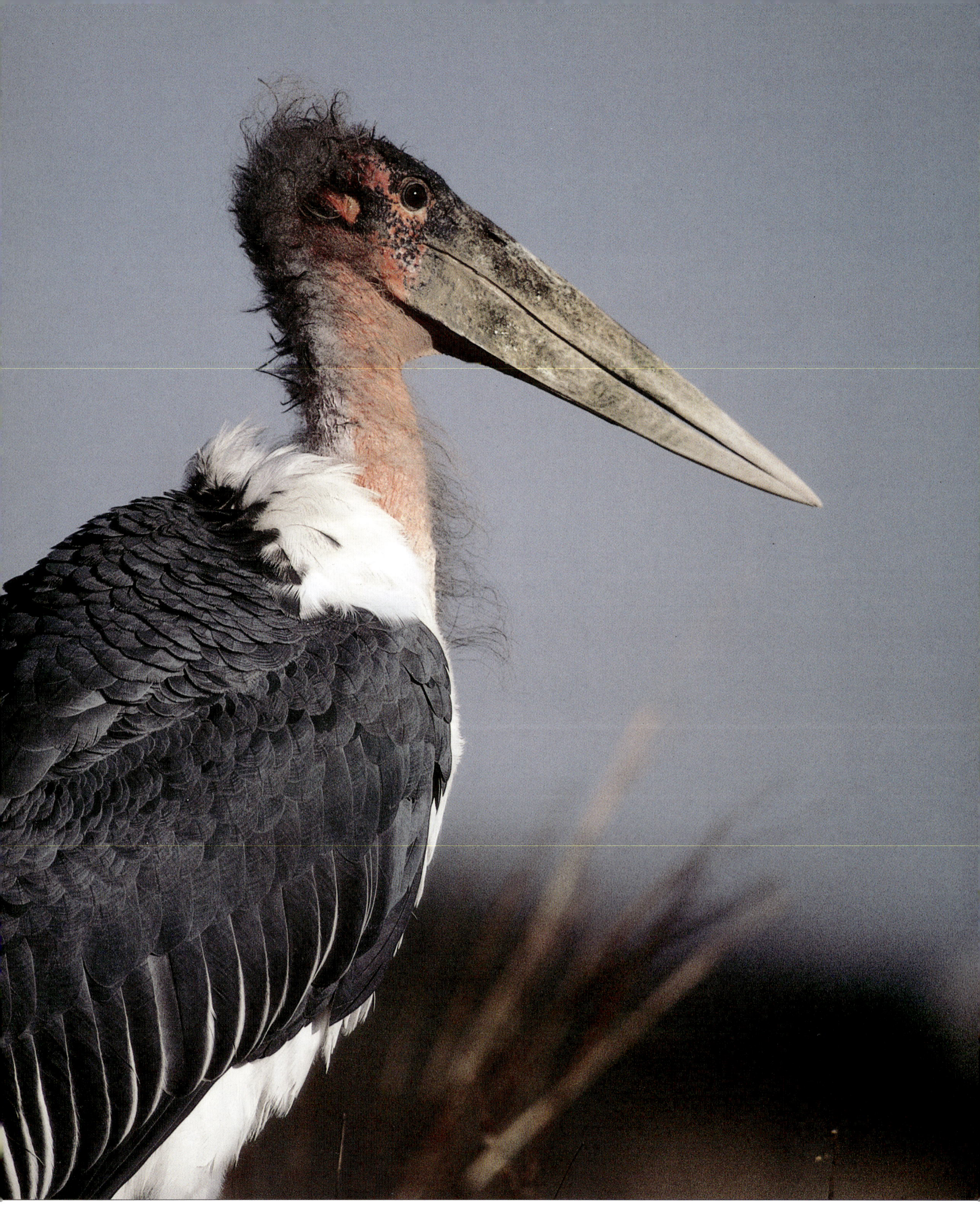

Few birds have more character than the homely marabou, acknowledged as the world's largest stork due to its enormous wingspan, which can reach 2.6 metres.

FEATHERED INHABITANTS

Even novice bird-watchers risk becoming avid ornithologists when confronted with the variety and hue of bird-life in Namibia. From stately storks to flashy flamingoes, from electric blues to fiery reds, from haughty runners to humble waders, the country's feathered inhabitants are surprisingly engaging. Southern Africa boasts more than 900 species of bird and many of these can be spotted in Namibia's woodland, thornveld, shrubland and desert habitats. After summer rains migrant species from the north swoop in to join the endemic species, creating huge flocks and a bird-lover's Eden.

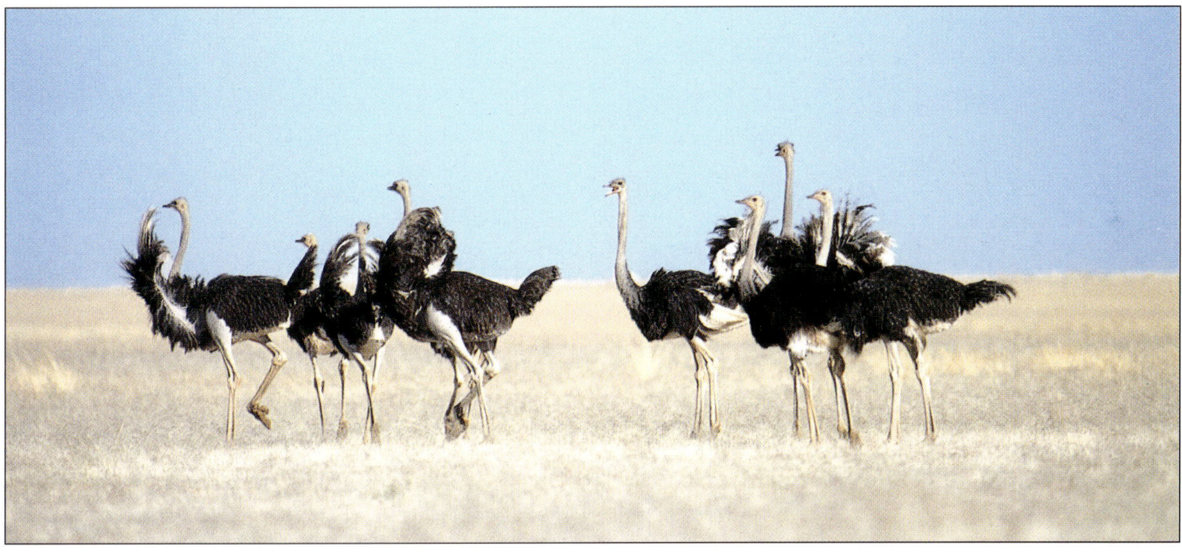

Easily flustered, ostriches bustle about the open plains of the Namib-Naukluft Park, no doubt frustrated at their inability to take to the air.

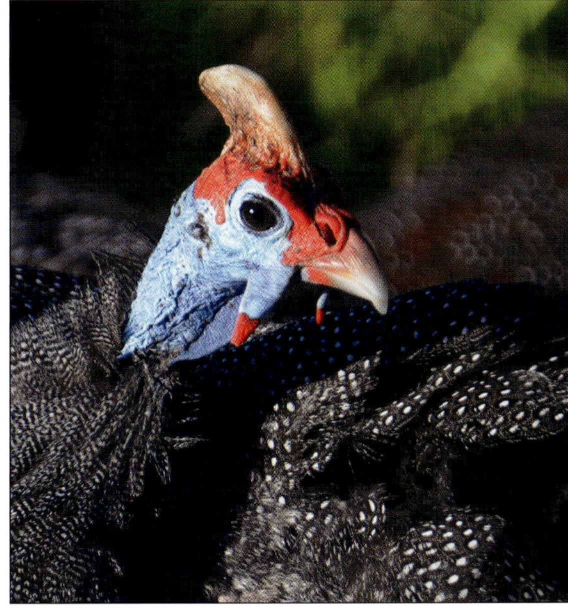

The helmeted guineafowl always appears to be in a hurry and is never alone.

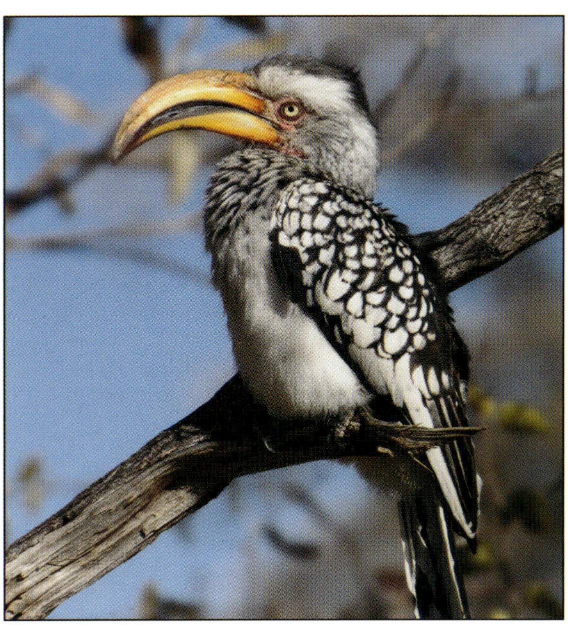

The southern yellowbilled hornbill is more friendly than he looks.

COLOUR AND CHARACTER

The crimsonbreasted shrike, a veritable jewel in any surroundings, is the country's national bird, while the iridescent glossy starling is one of its most common. Terrestrial types, such as the noble kori bustard - at 18 kilogrammes Africa's heaviest flying bird when it chooses to lift off - and the stately secretarybird, are frequently seen striding the open plains.

Wherever they are found, Namibia's birds have plenty of glamour and gloss, colour and character.

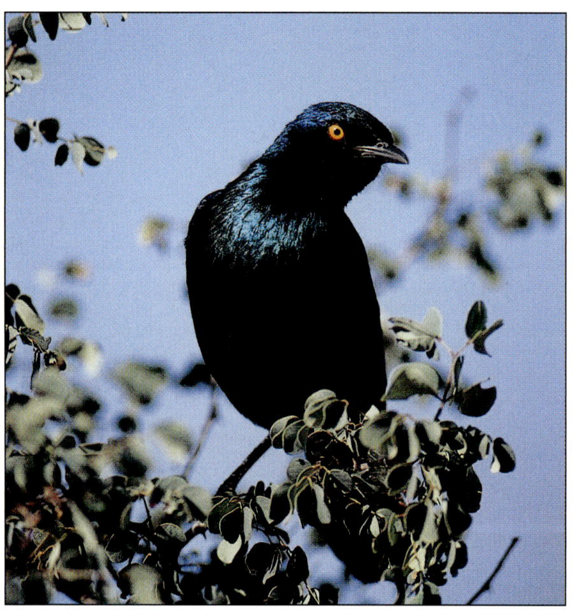

Glossy starling

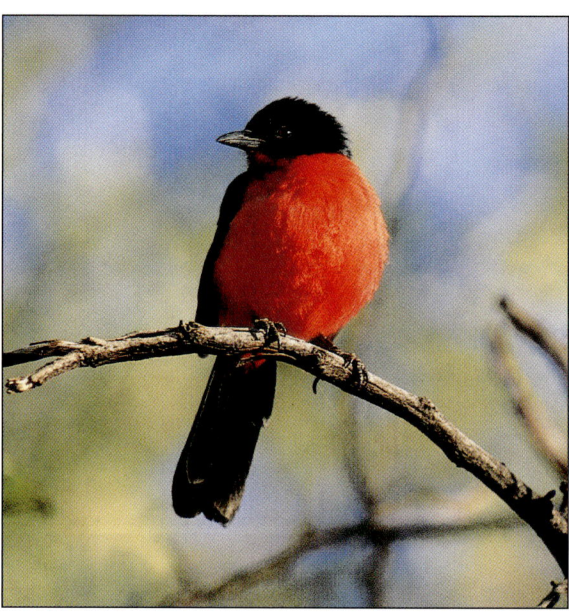

Crimsonbreasted shrike

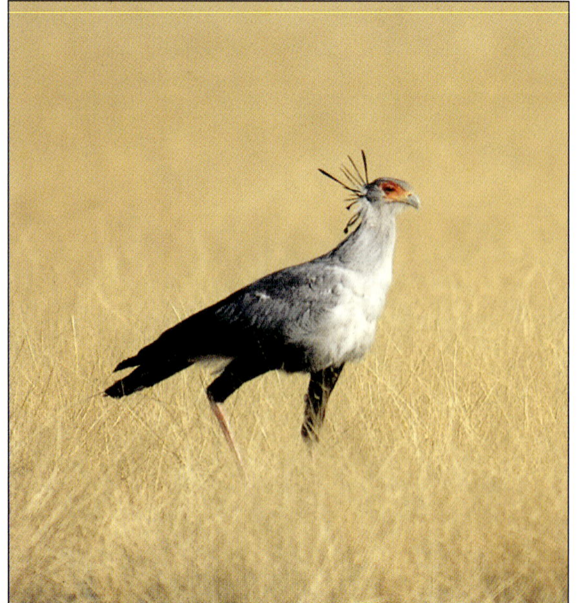

Secretarybird

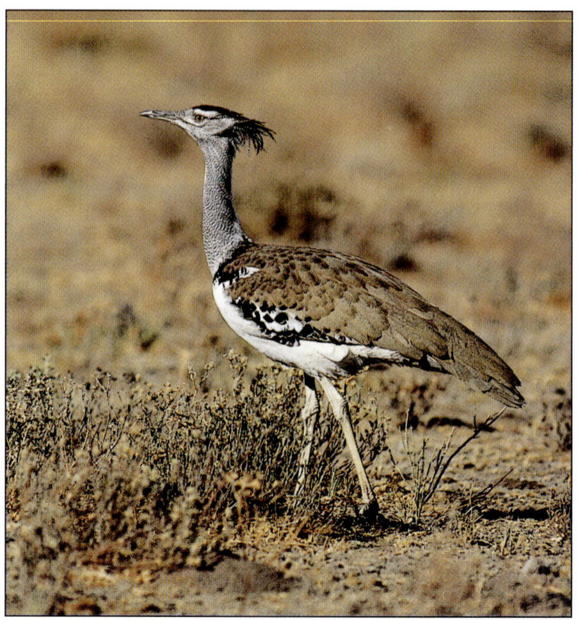

Kori bustard

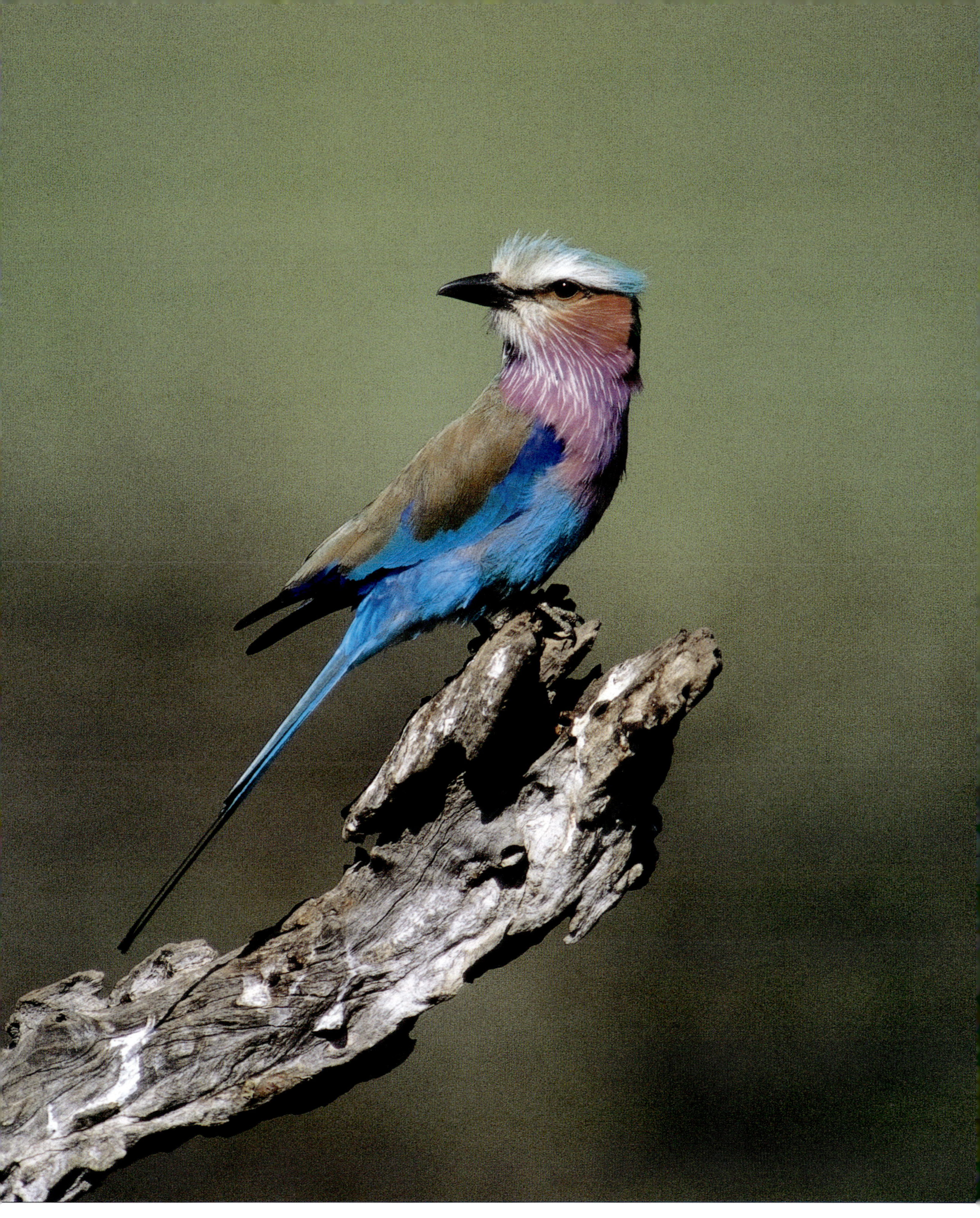

The exquisitely coloured lilacbreasted roller is a perennial favourite with visitors who thrill at the sight of mid-air flamboyance as male and female, alike, flash their brilliance.

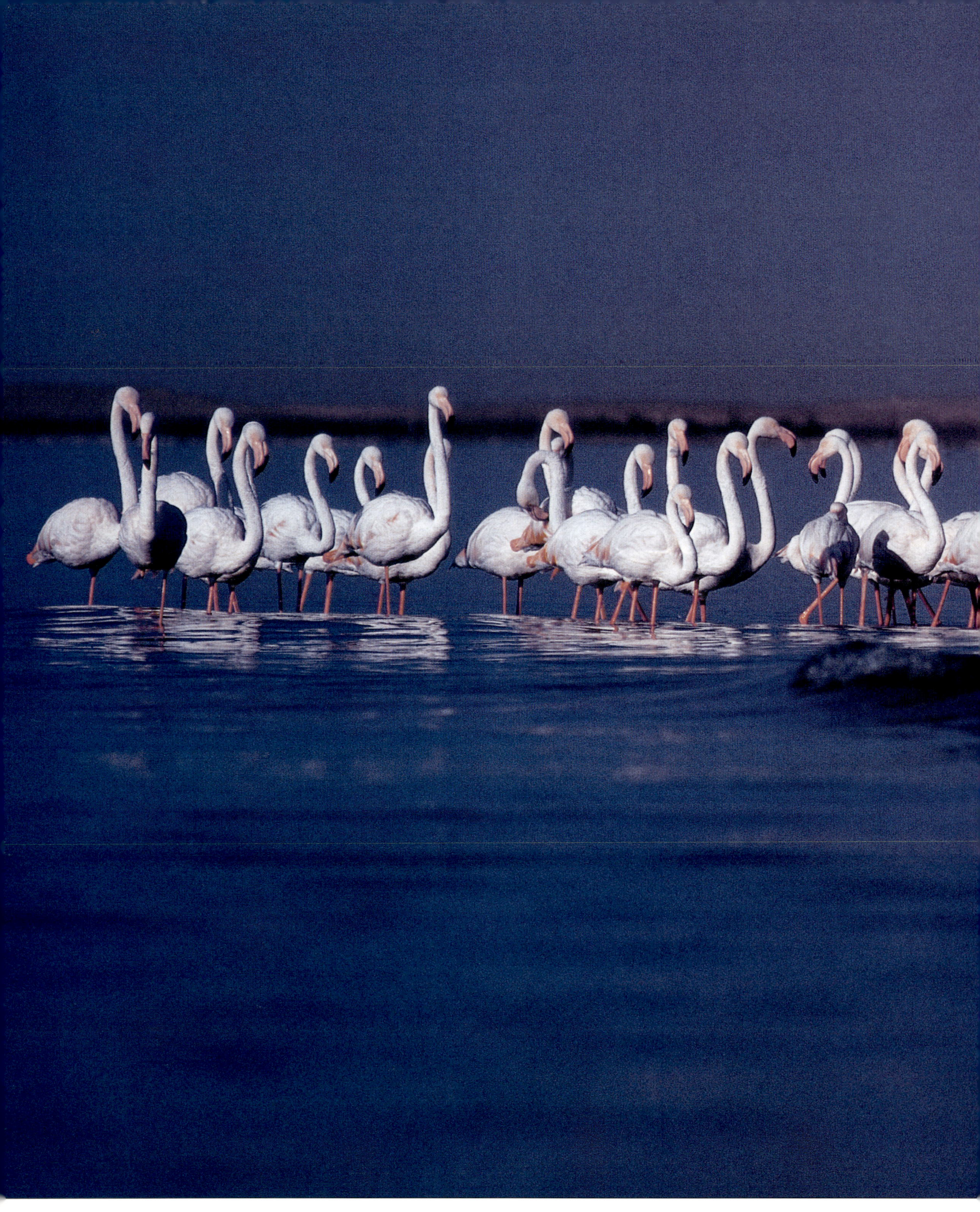

Flamingoes are a familiar sight at the lagoon in Walvis Bay. Both varieties, the greater – large and white with a pink bill, and the lesser – smaller and pink with dark bill, flock here in their thousands.

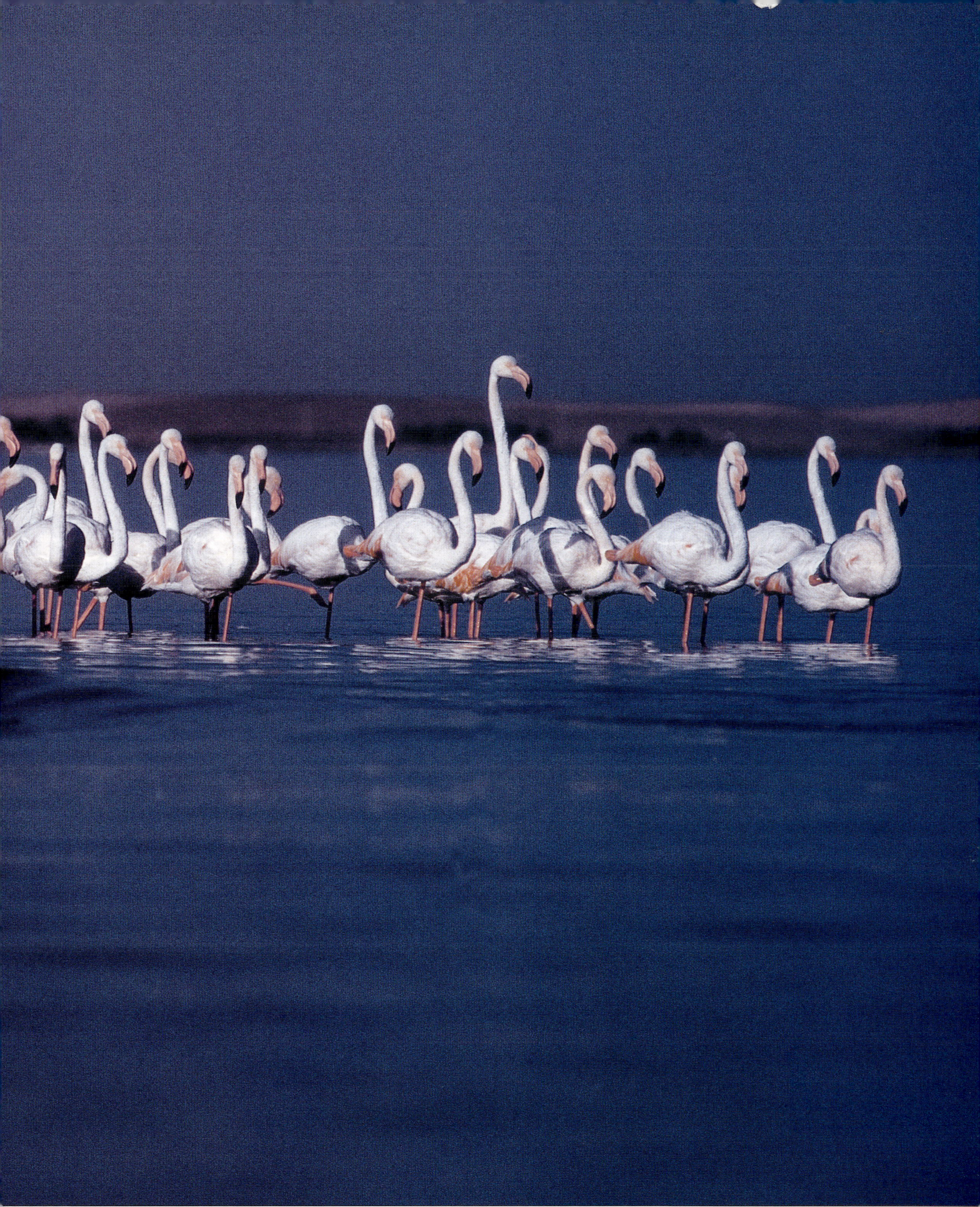

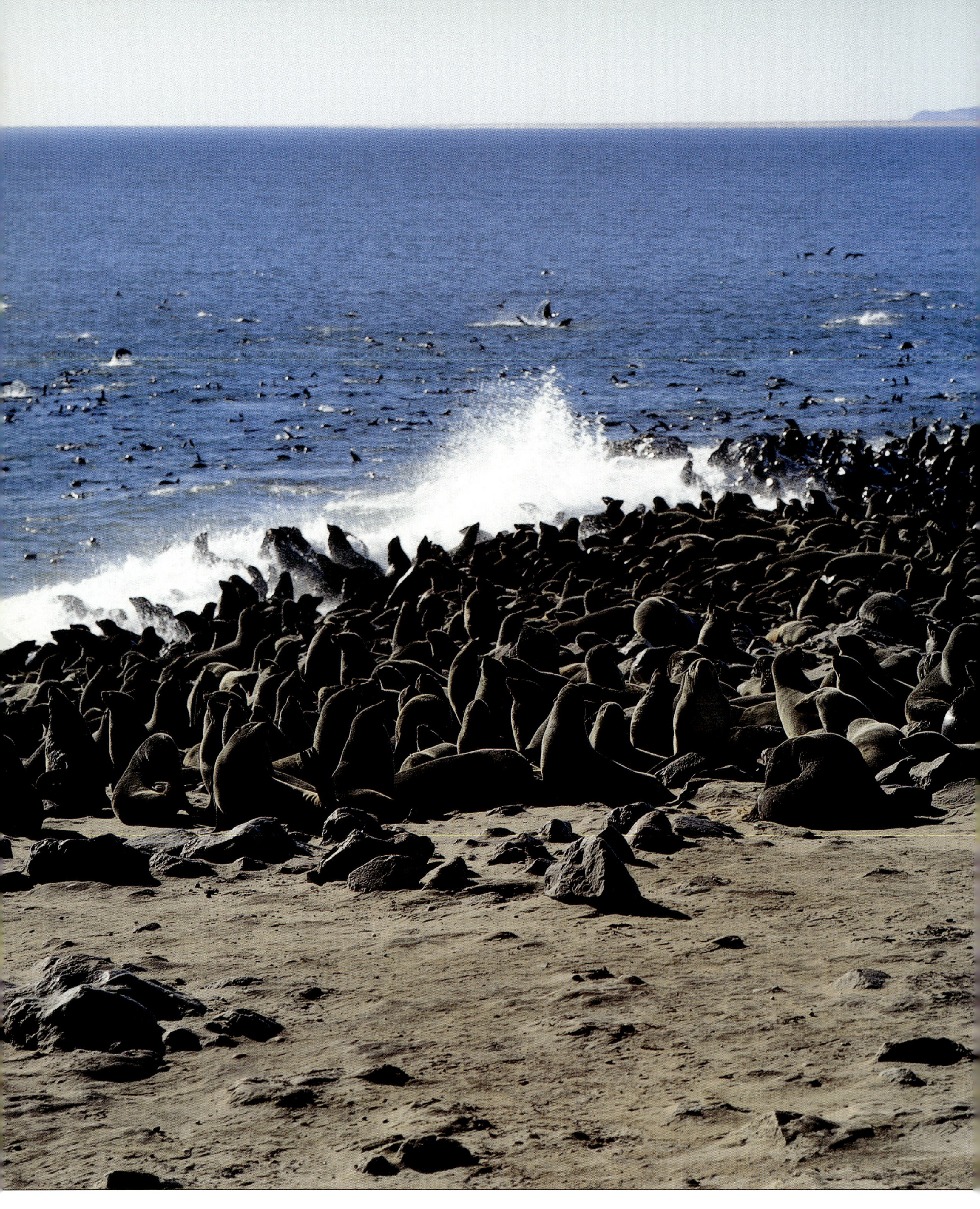

Cape Cross Reserve is a breeding colony for the Cape fur seals that flock ashore out of the icy Benguela current. A quick headcount at the colony reveals between 80,000 to 100,000 seals.

CAPE CROSS AND SEAL RESERVE

When Portuguese navigator-explorer Diego Câo battled his way through the angry Atlantic seas and clambered ashore at Cape Cross to erect a padrâo or stone cross on the hostile headland, he wasn't staking his claim to a seal colony. It was 1486 and Câo, the first European to set foot in Namibia, was simply fulfilling the orders of his Court to raise the cross on "new-found shores - in the name of Portugal, King John II and Christianity". Having failed on a previous mission, desperation to succeed on his second expedition drove him to settle for this unavailing, rocky promontory. Oblivious to the existence of the cross, no one took a blind bit of notice of its claim for the next 400 years or so until European sailing ships, scouring the seaboard for guano deposits, came across it. In 1893, the cross, battered by the elements, was removed to Germany and replaced with a wooden replica, which was later succeeded by the granite replica standing near the spot today.

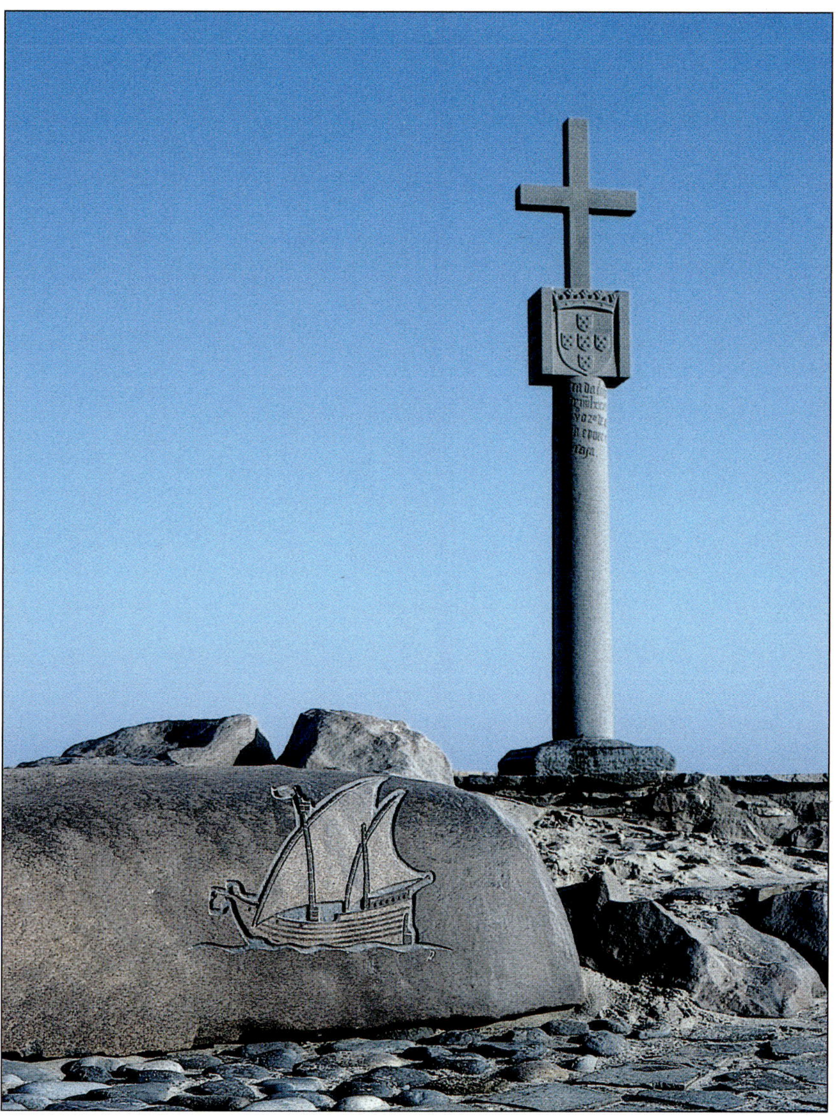

Kaiser Wilhem of Germany ordered this granite replica of the padrão that had been erected in 1486 by explorer Diego Cão.

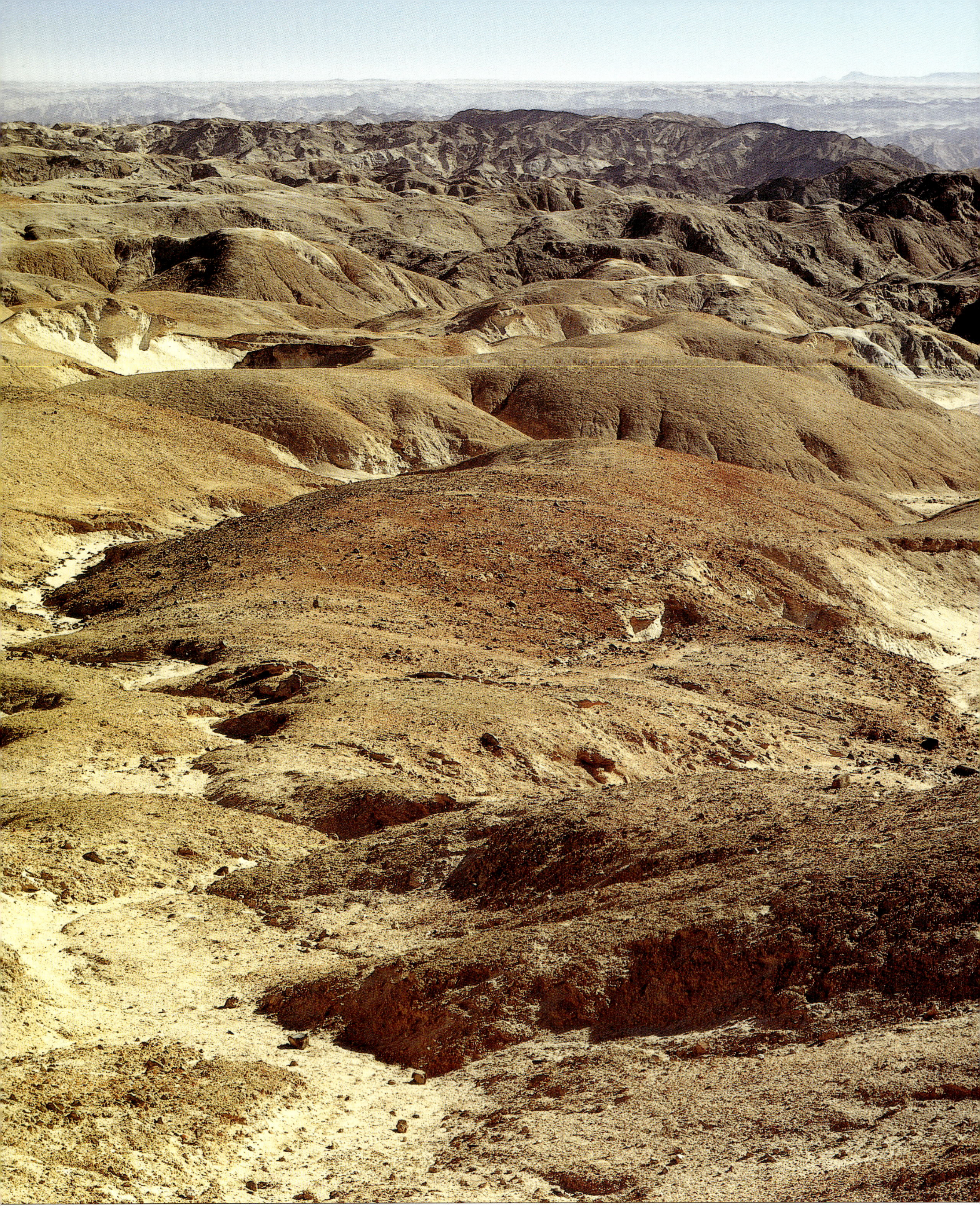

The lunar-like landscape near Swakopmund represents another fascinating chapter in the country's geological history. During rains, twisting rivulets course down the decline to the Swakop River.

MOONSCAPE AND MIRABILIS

The Namib-Naukluft Park abounds with natural wonders - such as the impressive lunar landscape of the Swakop River Valley. Around 460 million years ago during Namibia's mountain-building phase, the area's granite rocks rose from the earth's interior laying the foundations of the ancient Damara Mountains. Erosion over many more millions of years gnawed away at the high mountain chain eventually reducing it to low ridges. Over the past two million years, the Swakop River has caused further destruction in this area, creating the badland topography visible today. Granite is generally hard enough to withstand weathering but extreme variation in daytime temperatures and fog seeping into the upper layers of rock, leave the moonscape terrain more susceptible to erosion.

Another of the Park's ancient treasures is the primeval *Welwitschia Mirabilis*, one of the world's most unusual plants. Although officially classified as a tree related to both conifer and cycad, the welwitschia has the traits of a plant and behaves like a moss. Just two leaves sprout from a low-lying trunk but as these grow they intertwine and shred, spreading a clump of tattered and tired-looking bract across the Namib gravel. Discovered by Austrian botanist, Friedrich Welwitsch, in 1859, the plant has many idiosyncrasies. Although its root system can penetrate to 30 metres, the welwitschia absorbs fog through its leaf surface and distributes the moisture from there to the rest of the plant. The plant has distinct male and female specimens and, with remarkable longevity, can survive in this harsh environment for hundreds of years.

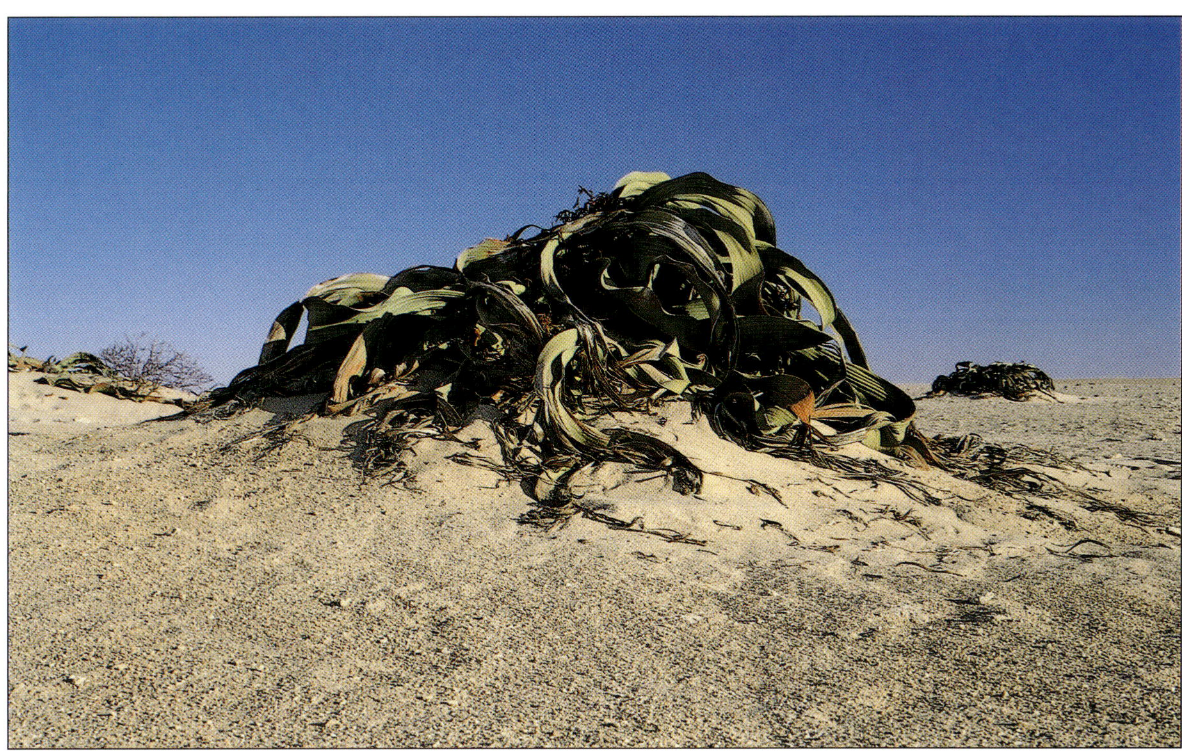

The weird Welwitschia Mirabilis is endemic to Namibia and Angola. The Welwitschia Drive near Swakopmund boasts many fine specimens, one estimated to be 1,500 years old.

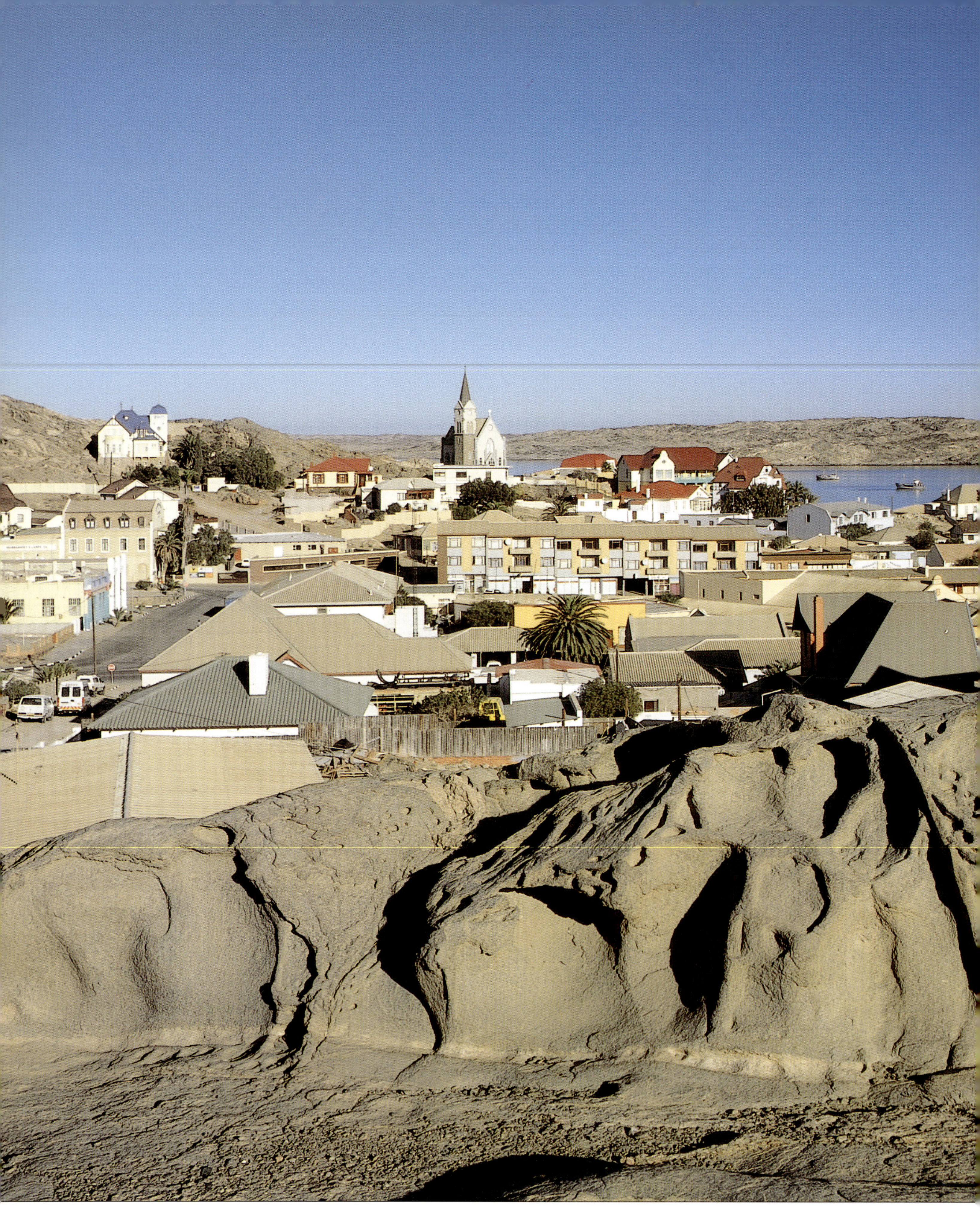

On the slopes of distant Diamantberg (Diamond Mountain) the imposing Goerke House looks out to the landmark spire of the Felsenkirche (Church on the Rocks).

COLONIAL CHARM IN COASTAL TOWNS

On 17 December 1920, the League of Nations officially ended the German Government's reign in Namibia. Yet nearly a century later the colonialist's influence still pervades the coastal towns of Lüderitz and Swakopmund.

Lüderitz, perched on Namibia's only rocky stretch of shoreline, was the first German settlement in the old Südwestafrika. Then, it was a bustling sea port frequented by merchants and diamond miners. The gracious Victorian-era buildings left behind when they departed seem oddly at home in this rocky, virtually treeless frontier, squashed between the mighty sand dunes of the Namib desert and the crashing waves of the Atlantic seaboard. Today the quaint fishing village is the centre of Namibia's rock lobster industry and the focal point of its diamond industry.

Lying lazily between two oceans - one of sea, the other of sand - the popular seaside resort of Swakopmund is a charming town of promenades, palm trees and ornate public buildings. Here, genteel colonial ambience permeates the atmosphere, from the Bavarian-style cafés and delicatessens to the graceful art noveau architecture of the 19th century that still characterises the town. Swakop, as it is fondly called, is a great base for exploring the unique landscapes of the Namib-Naukluft Park as well as the fishing and recreational playgrounds of the rugged Atlantic Coast.

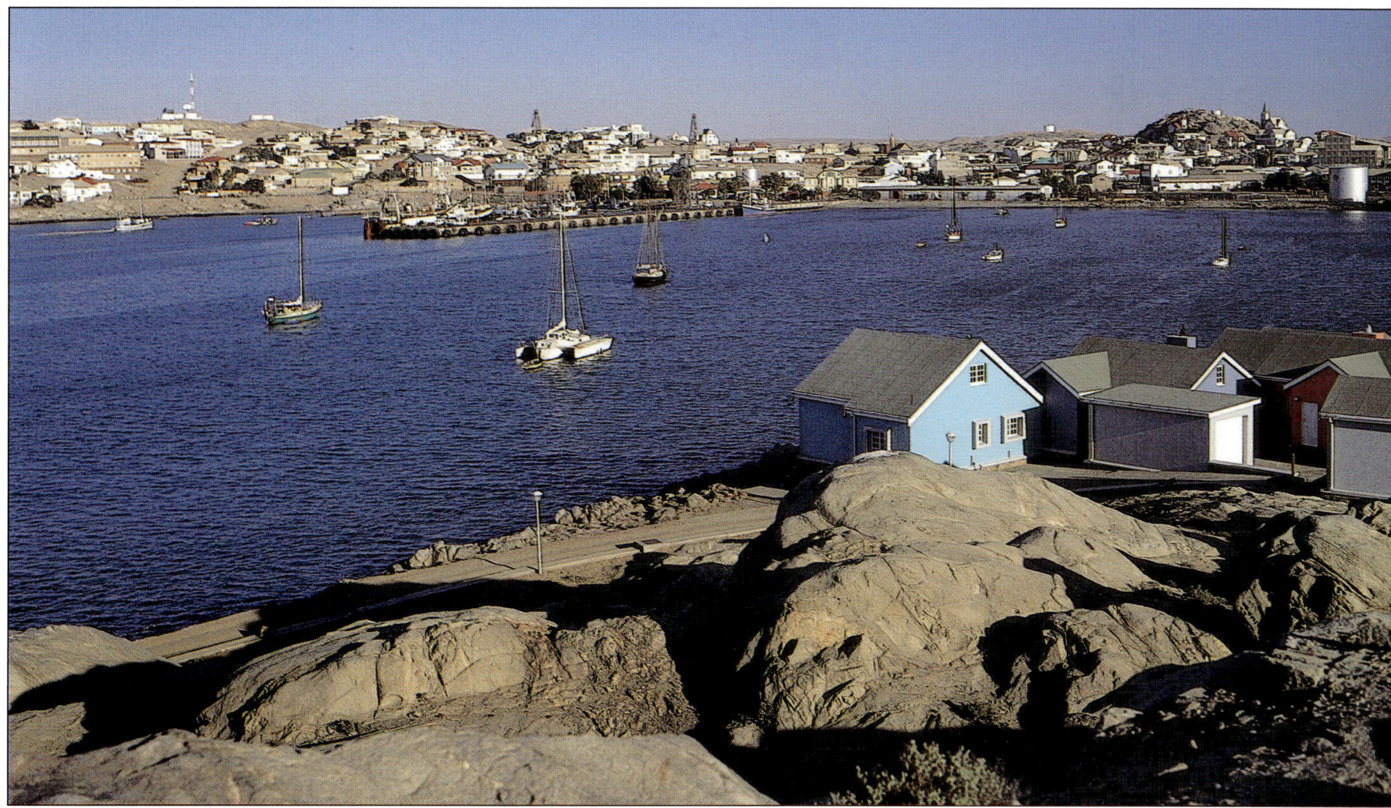

Shark Island, once adrift in the bay but now joined to the mainland by a solid causeway, provides a commanding view over Lüderitz for visitors at its municipal restcamp.

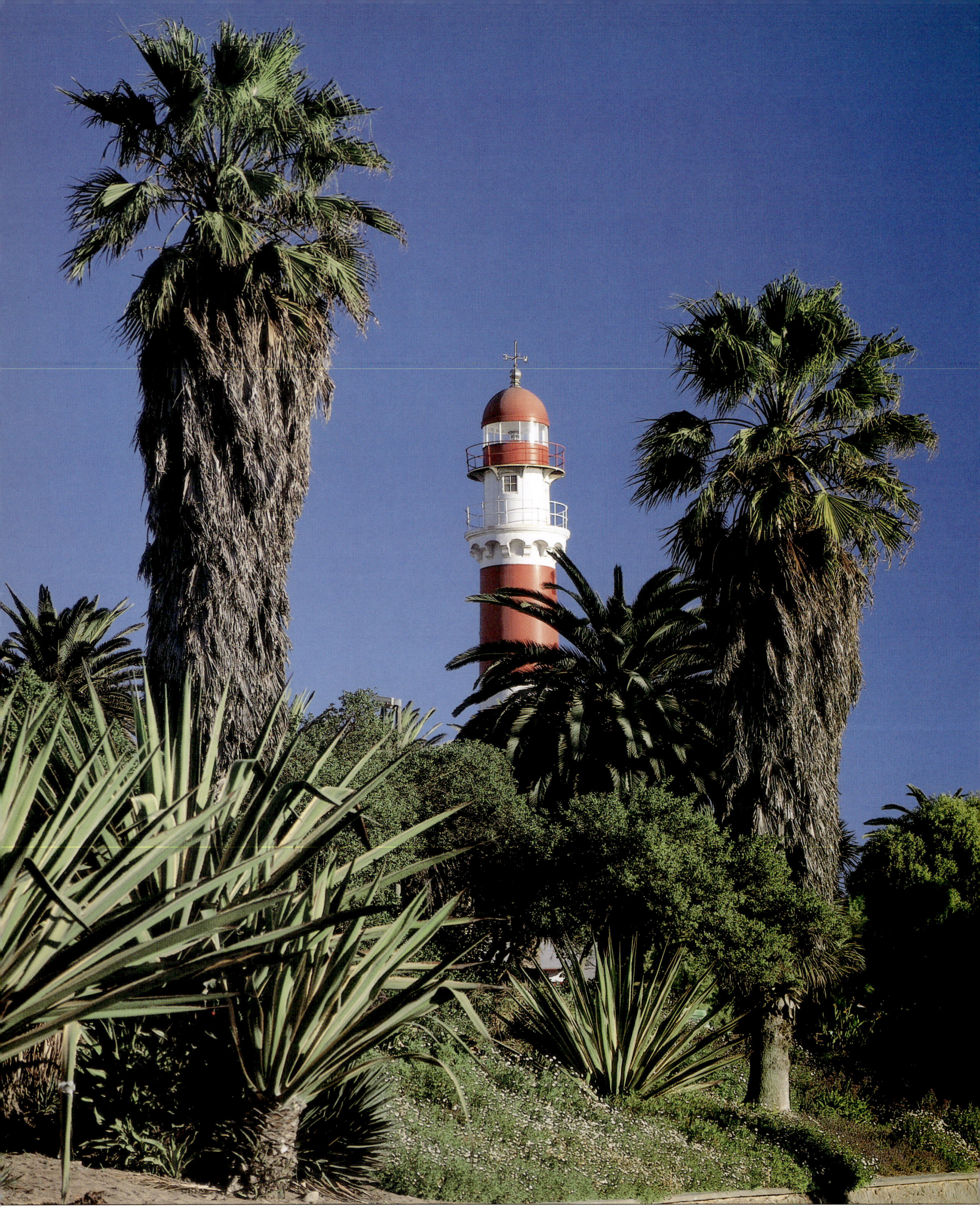

The 20-metre slimline lighthouse, erected in 1902 to guide sailors into Swakopmund's challenging port, was mission impossible. The harbour waters proved too shallow for ships to dock.

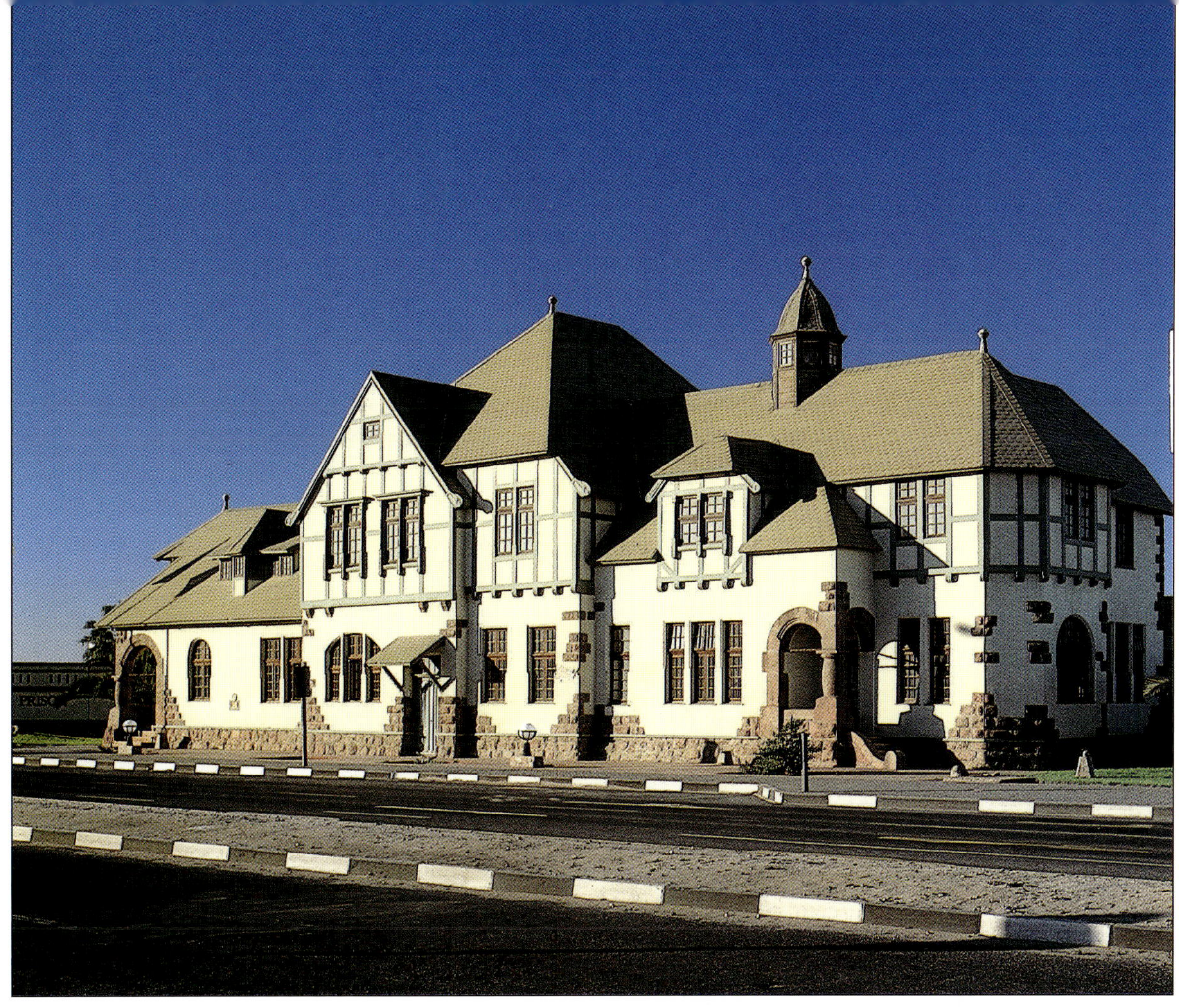

Swakopmund's graceful architecture is not confined to sophisticated pursuits. Even the local penitentiary, built in 1909, exudes style and elegance.

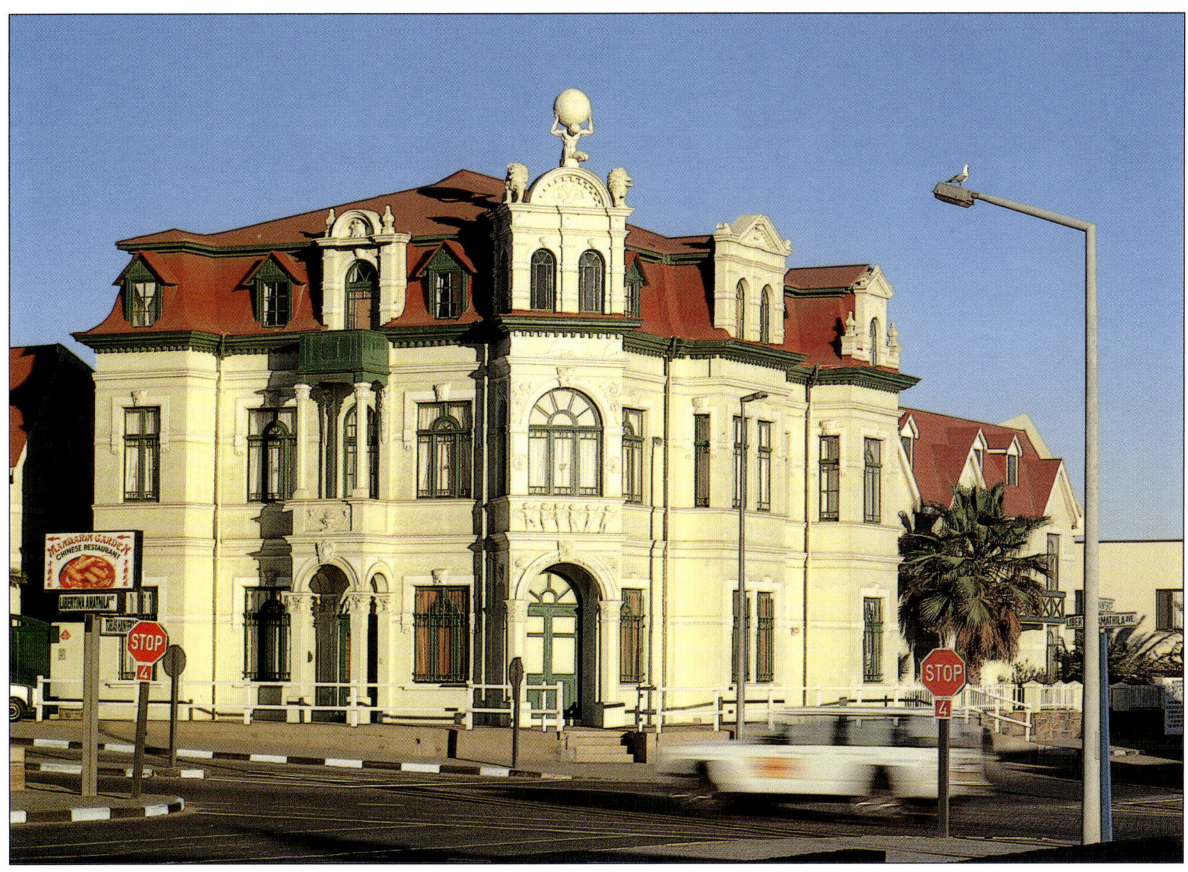

The magnificent Hohenzollernhaus (1906), with its elaborate mouldings and statue of Atlas, is one of Swakopmund's finest architectural treasures.

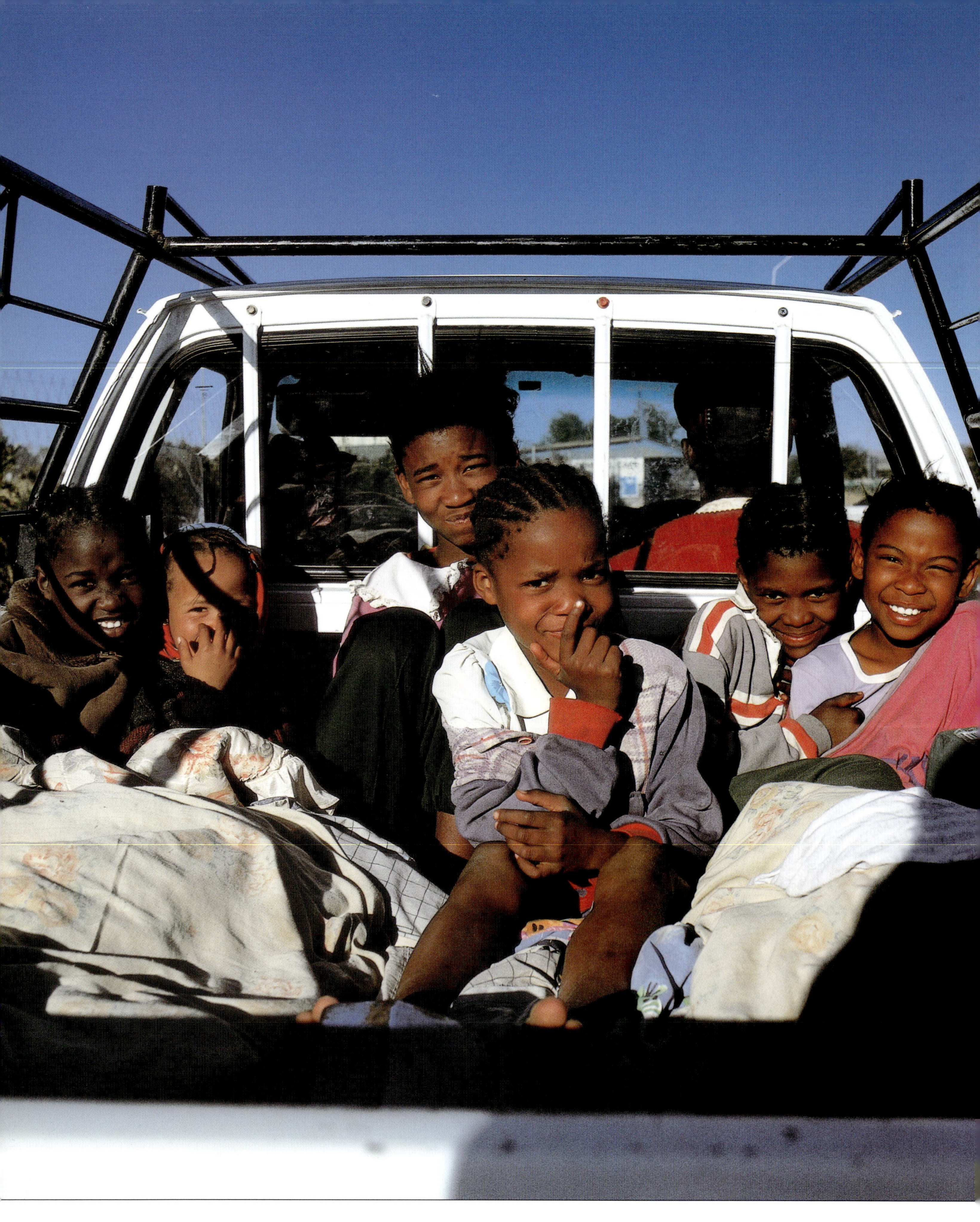

The flat-deck truck ('bakkie'), overflowing with passengers, is an everyday feature on the country's highways and byways. The happy Gariseb family use blankets to control the air-conditioning.

OUT AND ABOUT

Namibia has one of the lowest population densities in the world. In fact, if the country's inhabitants were evenly dispersed, there would be fewer than two people sharing each square kilometre. So it is not surprising that being out and about in the countryside is often akin to being all alone in the Universe. At times there is no sign of life or habitation as far as the eye can see until, out of nowhere, a solitary springbok strays, or maybe a gemsbok or two. Even more curious is the lonely pedestrian spied travelling a path that seems to come from nowhere and lead to nowhere. For much of the year dramatically blue heavens arch overhead toward boundless horizons, embracing the landscape between and heightening the tranquillity that fills the vacant expanse.

Around two thirds of the population still live in rural areas where informal and communal farming is widely practiced. Vegetation is sparse over wide tracts of the countryside where hardy Afrikaner, Brahman, and Simmentaler cattle graze alongside donkeys and horses. Dorper and Karakul sheep mingle with Angora and Boergoats, and shepherds are often encountered waiting patiently while their roaming flocks forage for food.

Donkey carts are a familiar mode of transport in rural areas, with their modern day counterpart – the flat-deck truck - becoming increasingly popular, especially near the urban areas.

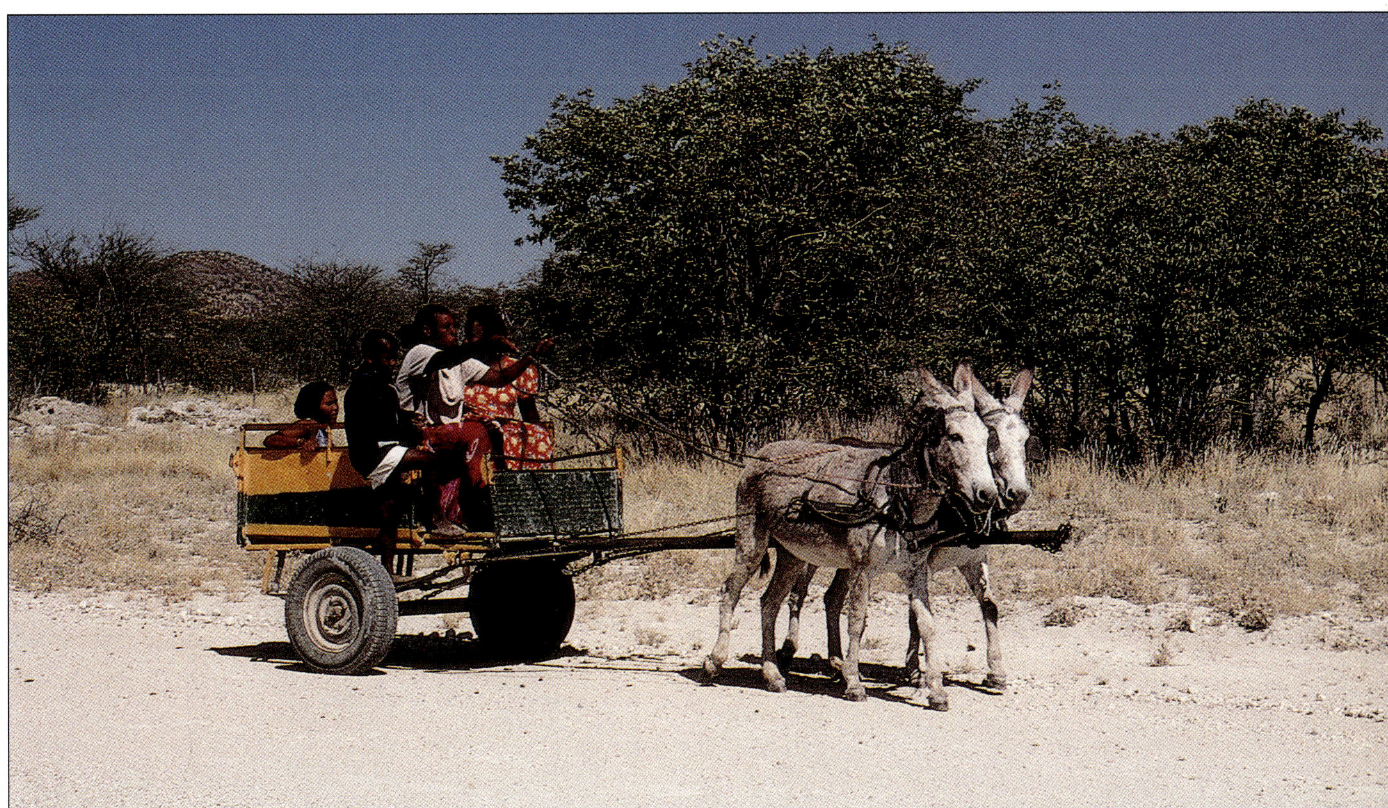

No twin overhead cam, power steering or fuel injection. It may take a while, but at least this happy bunch have plenty of time to take in the scenery on their outing to Khorixas.

WINDHOEK - CAPITAL CITY

Namibia's only designated city, Windhoek, is also the capital. It is fittingly dotted in the middle of the country, in a high-lying mountain valley. Though small in population, it is a thoroughly cosmopolitan city - a cultural melting pot where colourful African meets classic colonial and vibrant contemporary, a lively city with much to offer tourists.

Windhoek's first significant role was as a garrison for the German military in the late nineteenth century. The early European atmosphere remains an intrinsic part of the city's modern-day character, particularly in the bustling main thoroughfare of Independence Avenue. Here colonial façades snuggle comfortably below multi-storey steel and glass edifices to give the tree-lined boulevard a relaxed charm, despite its proximity to the cut and thrust of the central business district. A medley of continental cafés, museums and markets adds to the city's appeal.

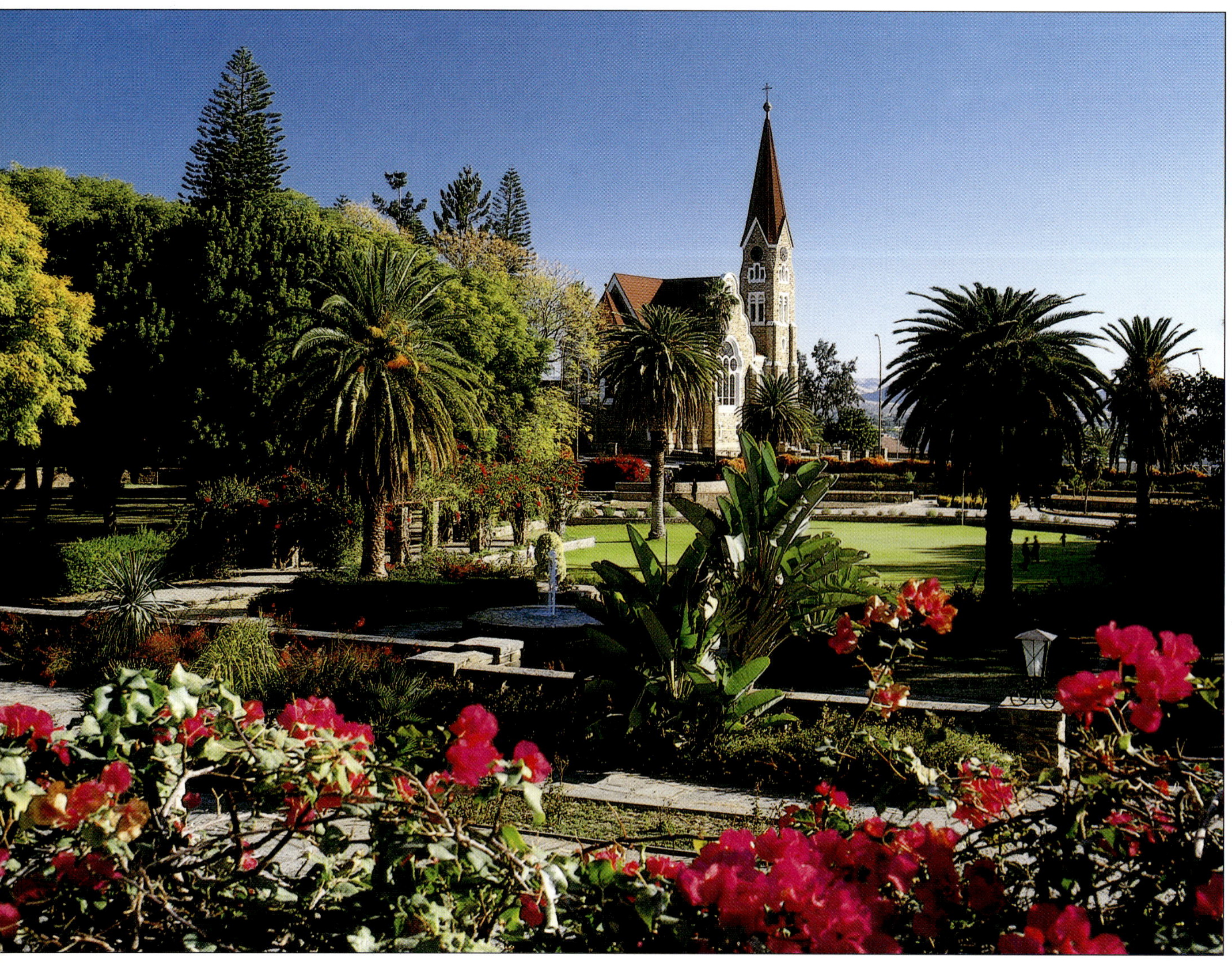

The gardens of the Tintenpalast (Ink Palace), seat of Namibia's Parliament, offer a restful view to the Christuskirche, a monument to peace built by the German Evangelical community.

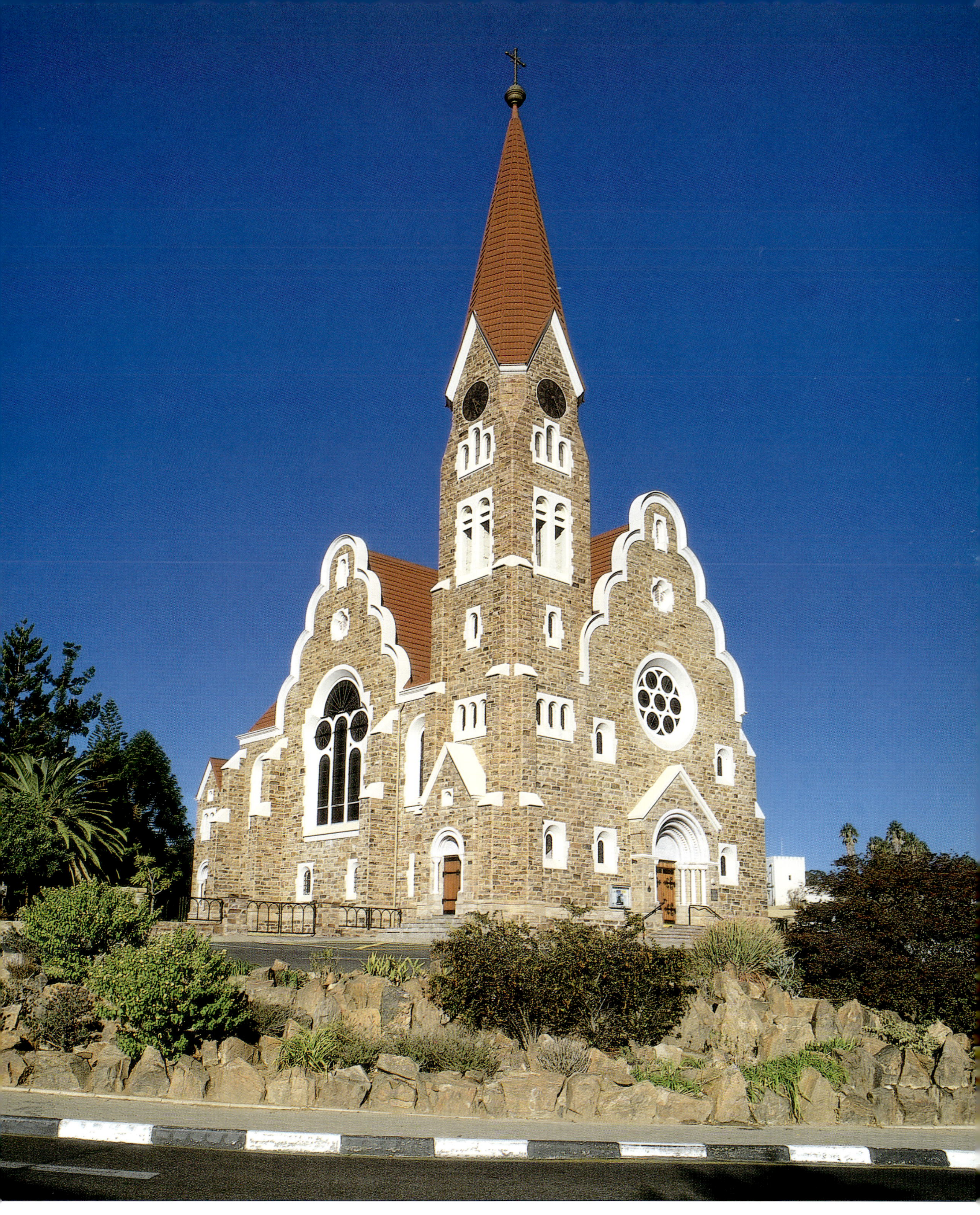

The sandstone Christuskirche (Church of Christ), built in 1910 in an eclectic blend of neo-Romanesque, art noveau and Gothic architecture, stands proudly on the hill overlooking Windhoek.

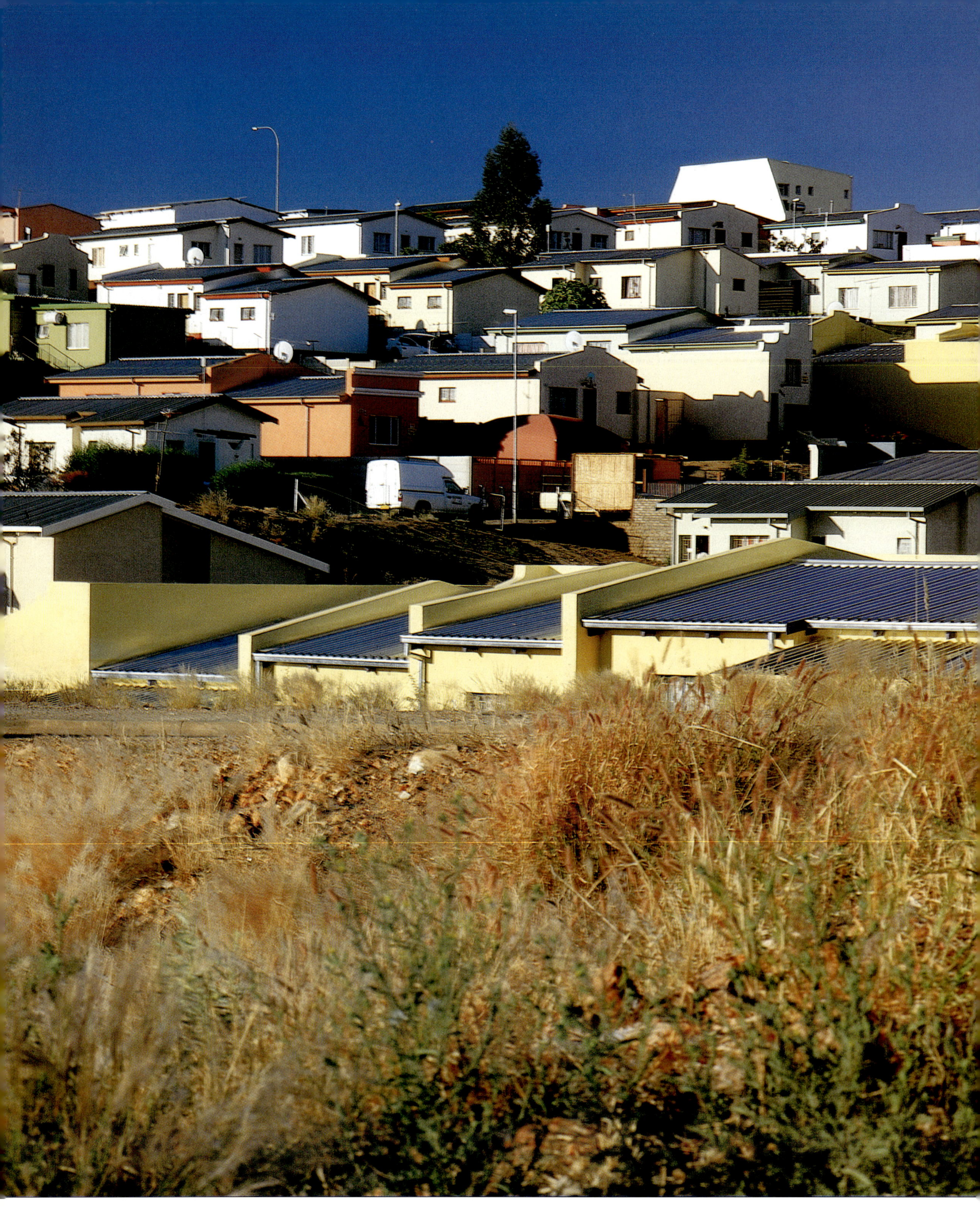

Dorado Park is reminiscent of modern suburbs around the world. It sits clean and cheerful on one of the numerous hillsides that accommodate Windhoek's urban sprawl.

A MODERN COUNTRY

Windhoek, along with most of Namibia's major towns, has all the amenities of a modern and thriving country. Hotels, shops and restaurants mingle with businesses, banks and services. In older towns, proud examples of colonial architecture reflect Namibia's early history, while across the country contemporary buildings echo trends found in many a burgeoning community throughout the world.

Since Namibia achieved independence in 1990, the young republic's past influences have been successfully integrated with its present-day aspirations to allow the momentum of progress to build in the twenty-first century. Democratically-elected governments have established political and social stability while pursuing objectives for sustained economic development that will provide better living standards for all citizens. Continuous improvement to crucial infrastructures such as transport, energy and communications enhances the potential for social and economic growth.

The country is a multi-ethnic land peopled by many races. Basta and Herero, Himba and Nama, Owambo and San, together with the many European descendants and migrants from east and west, have created a vibrant society with a sense of purpose, a nation of people proud to be Namibian.

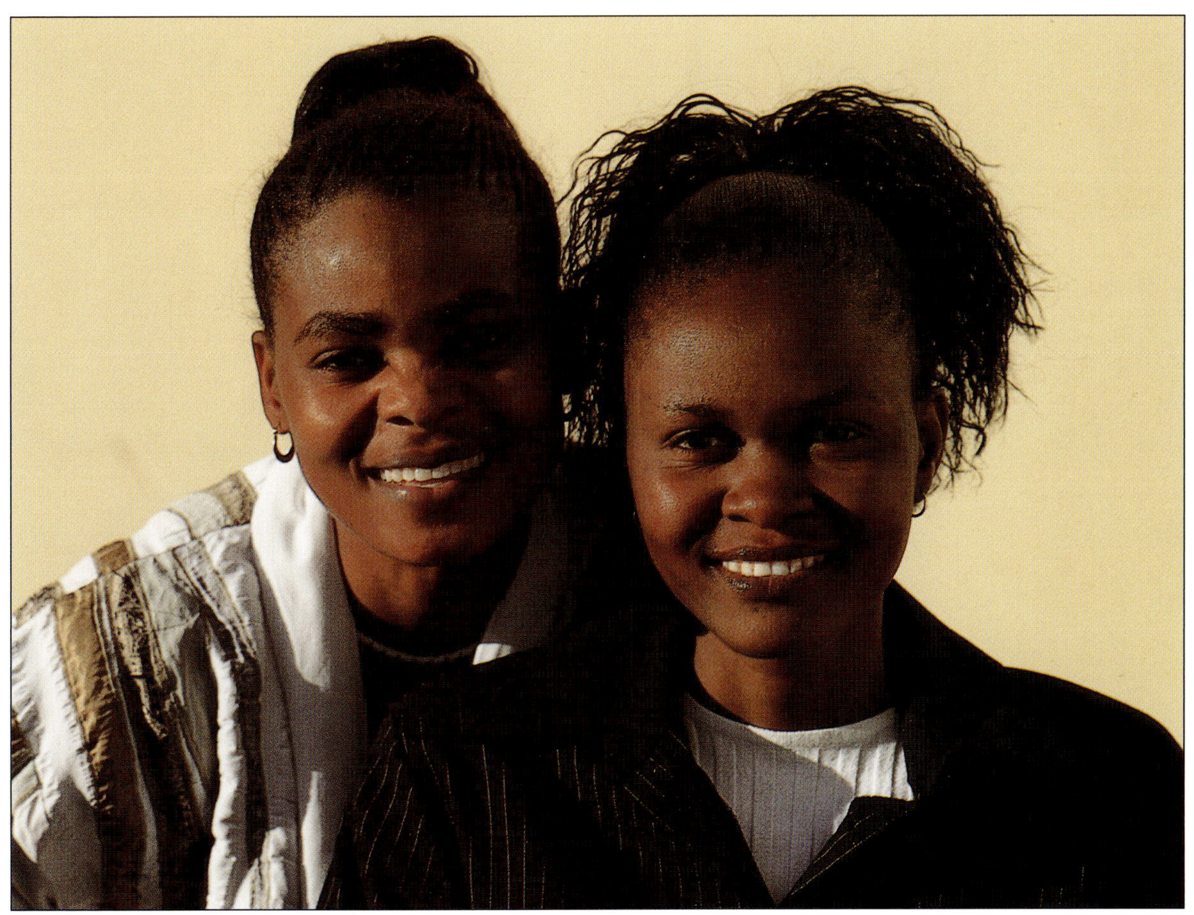

Young workers, Anna and Kristofina, hail from the Owambo hearth in Damaraland but work in the capital city. Almost two thirds of the population still live in rural areas.

NAMIBIA - A SPECTACULAR JOURNEY

There is a power and might about Namibia that is experienced on many of the journeys through its landscape. The treasure-mapped Welwitschia Drive near Swakopmund, the solitary drive from Sesriem to Sossusvlei, the forbidding terrain of the *Sperrgebeit*, the remote and tortured Skeleton Coast Park, the endless, restless yet restful Namib Desert, even the sedate drive along the coast from Swakopmund to Walvis Bay – they all have a compelling attraction and leave an indelible mark on the soul. And the fascination doesn't end when you reach your destination. It starts all over again with magnificent soaring dunes at Sossusvlei, teeming herds of wildlife at Etosha and flamingoes in their thousands at Walvis Bay lagoon; with breath-taking chasms at Fish River Canyon, the metallic, other-worldly surface of the 60 tonne Hoba meteorite, and the deafening surf and tossed up ship skeletons on the Atlantic seaboard. Or just with the thrill of sitting in awe, under the fairy-lit night sky at a campsite in the Namib, and counting shooting stars.

Nothing quite prepares visitors for what they encounter as they travel through Namibia – magic and mysteries, brilliance and bleakness, hardships and heroics. Above all, there is infinite colour. It is, quite simply, a spectacular journey.

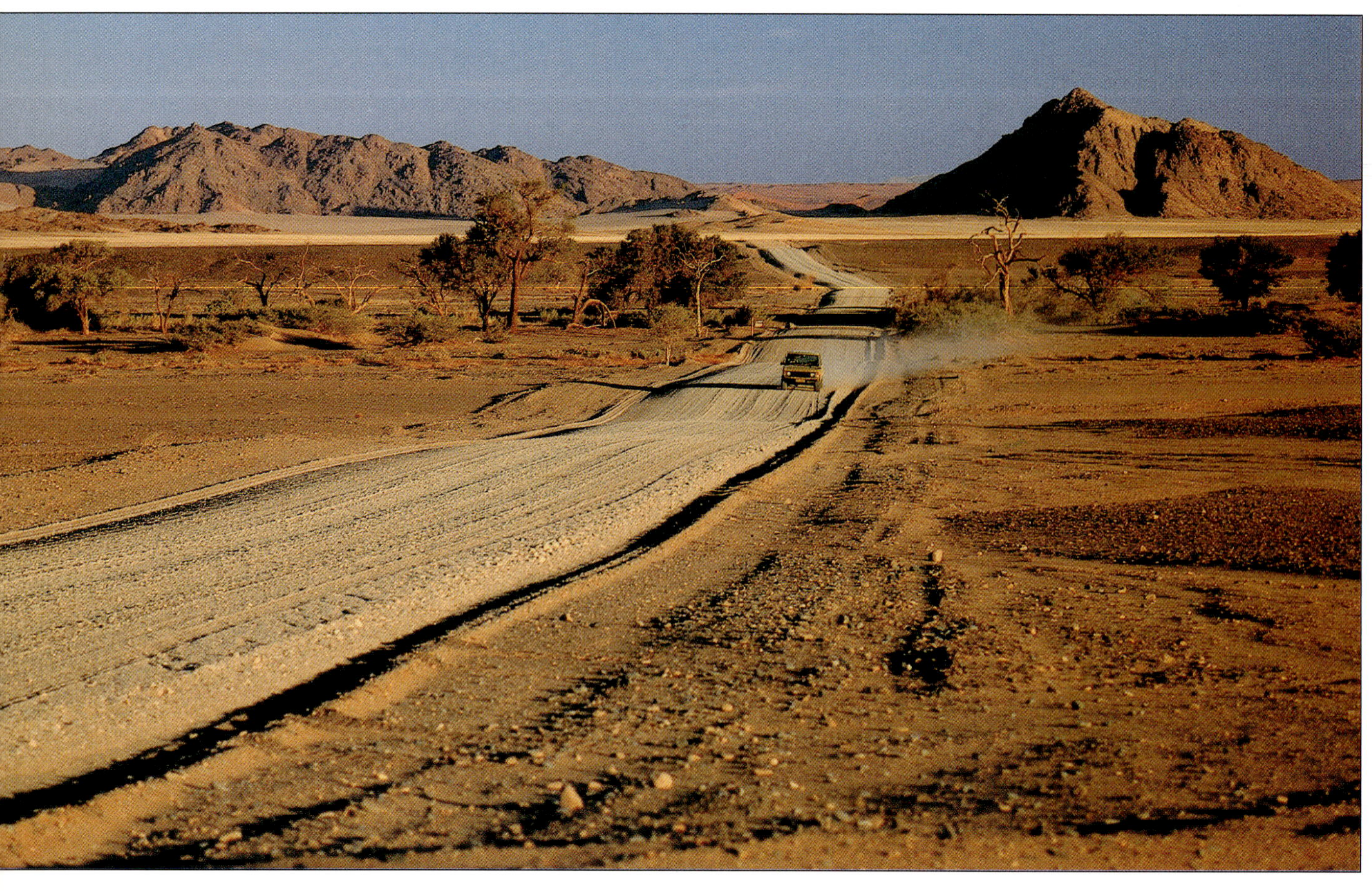

To journey through Namibia is to journey through extraordinary landscape - landscape that stirs the senses, touches the soul and calls you back again and again.

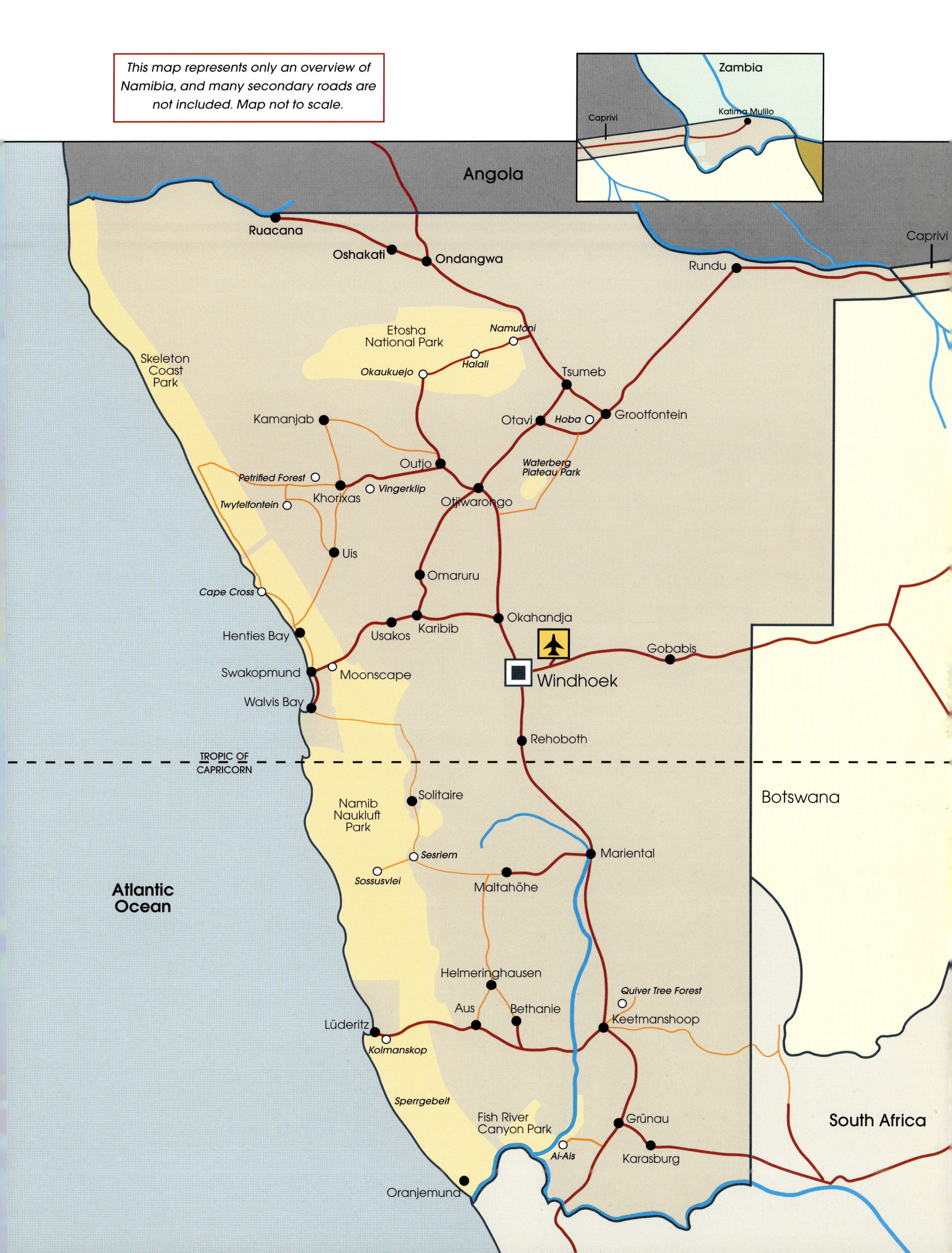
This map represents only an overview of Namibia, and many secondary roads are not included. Map not to scale.
Zambia
Caprivi
Katima Mulilo
Angola
Caprivi
Ruacana
Oshakati
Ondangwa
Rundu
Etosha National Park
Namutoni
Halali
Okaukuejo
Skeleton Coast Park
Tsumeb
Kamanjab
Otavi
Hoba
Grootfontein
Outjo
Waterberg Plateau Park
Petrified Forest
Vingerklip
Khorixas
Twyfelfontein
Otjiwarongo
Uis
Omaruru
Cape Cross
Okahandja
Usakos
Karibib
Henties Bay
Gobabis
Swakopmund
Moonscape
Windhoek
Walvis Bay
Rehoboth
TROPIC OF CAPRICORN
Solitaire
Botswana
Namib Naukluft Park
Mariental
Sesriem
Sossusvlei
Maltahöhe
Atlantic Ocean
Helmeringhausen
Quiver Tree Forest
Aus
Bethanie
Keetmanshoop
Lüderitz
Kolmanskop
Sperrgebeit
Fish River Canyon Park
Grünau
South Africa
Ai-Ais
Karasburg
Oranjemund

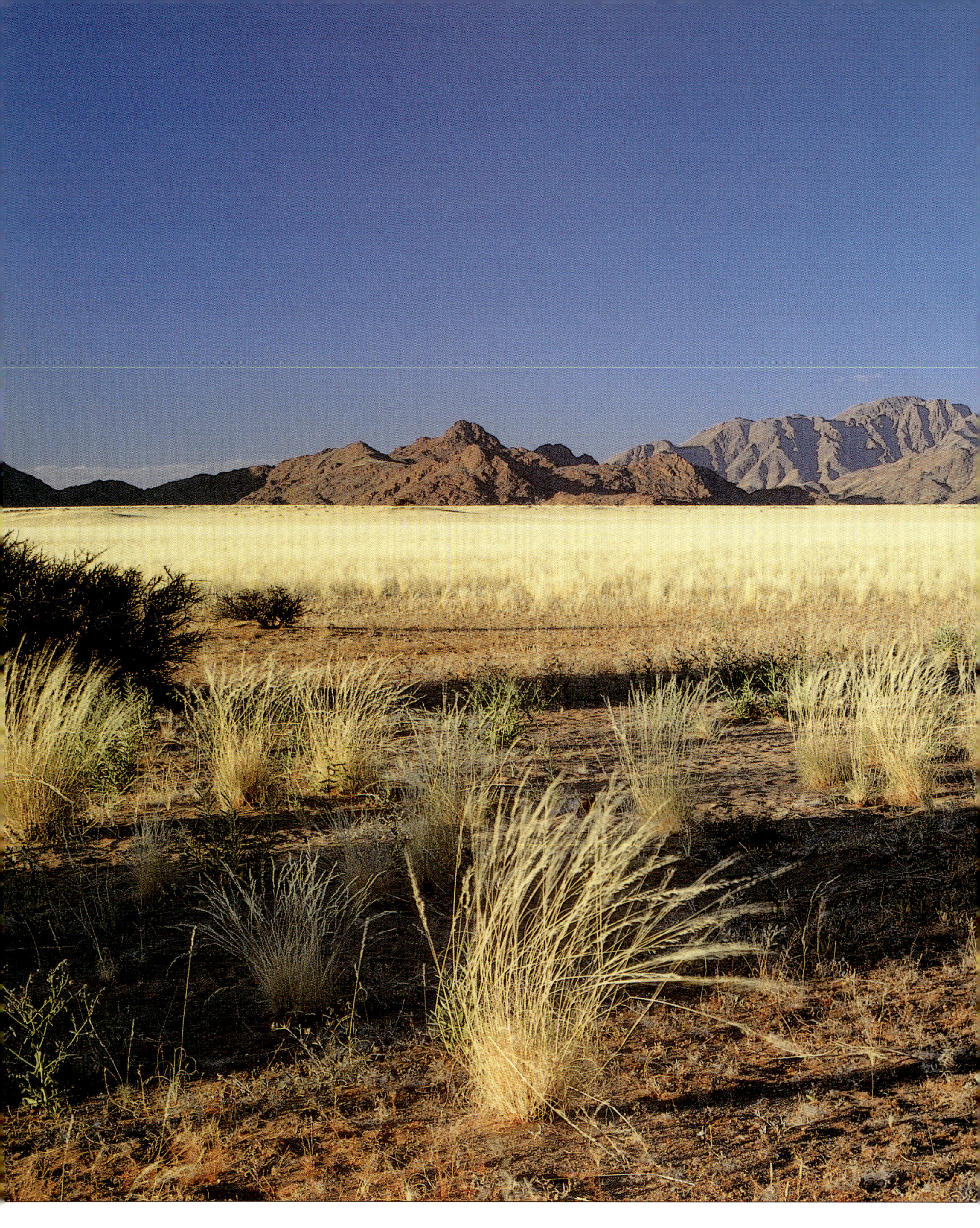

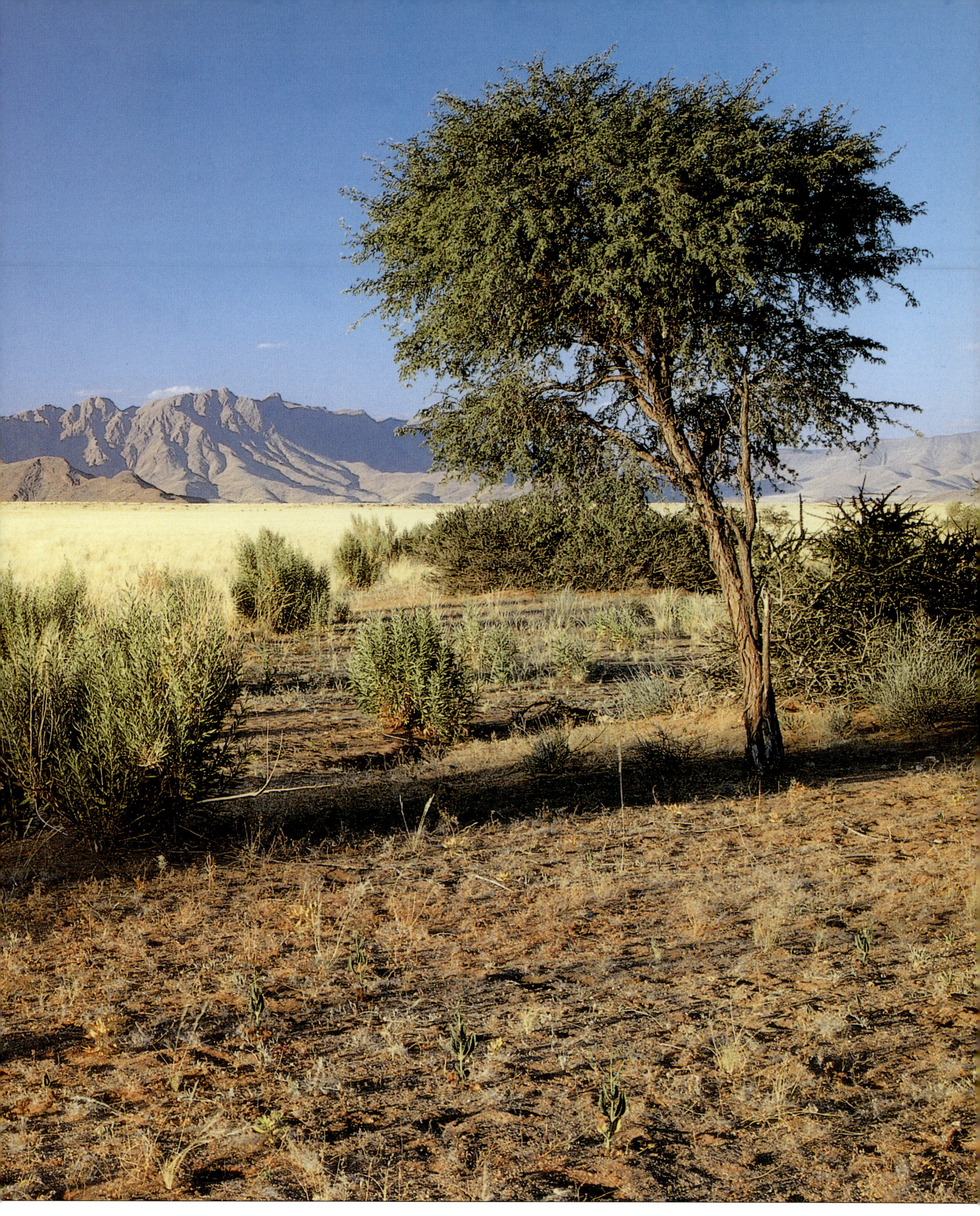

Early morning sunlight warms this late winter tableau near Sesriem. Softly tinted grasses stretch across the plains to merge with the rich, craggy textures of the distant Naukluft Mountains.

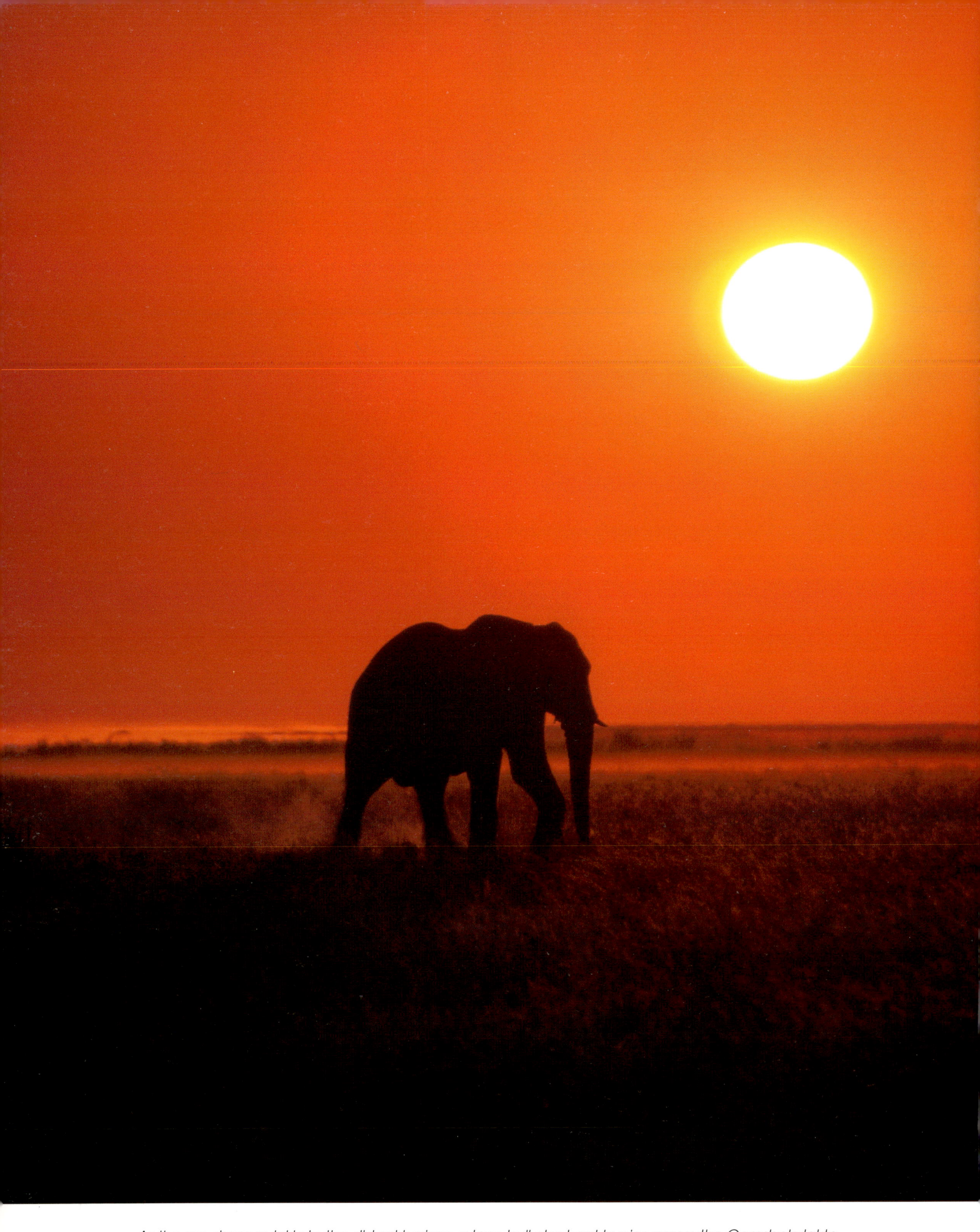

As the sun drops quickly to the distant horizon, a lone bull elephant hurries across the Gemsbokvlakte plains in anticipation of a twilight thirst quencher at the local waterhole.